WHY FREEDOM

Amber,

I loved spending time with you — I hope we get a chance to do so again soon...

Always,

1/2003

WHY FREEDOM

The Meaning and Practice of Freedom

Jason A. Junge

609-JUNG

To order additional copies of this book, contact:
Xlibris Corporation
1-888-7-XLIBRIS
www.Xlibris.com
Orders@Xlibris.com

CONTENTS

PART THREE:

External Currents

This book is dedicated to my mother and father, Kurt and Cristina, for their endless support and open minds; to my sister Diana, for always having faith in me; and to my friend Dr. Odysseas Kostas, for all his help and influence. I would also like to thank my editor Susan Malone for her valuable insight.

Introduction

A World of Regret

All of our lives are tied to a unique portion of space and time in the history of the universe. Anything and everything that we do is irreversibly set in historical stone—a stone that is completely unique to each one of us. Among the many facets that make us, our history and experiences are of paramount importance. We are in essence creating ourselves through our experiences and history with each decision. This knowledge of creative irreversibility and uniqueness gives every decision infinite significance, creating anguish over making the right choice in light of uncertainty. This sense of responsibility arises from our ownership of pens with which we write the history of not only our own unique lives, but also a portion of the history of mankind.

Looking back, we all have faced those forks in the road where for whatever reason, we made the wrong choices. We picked these majors in college instead of those; these girls or boys were not pursued in high school and it turns out they were probably interested in us; we did not take the opportunity to pass a resume along at the right time; or we gave up playing the piano and now regret it. Life is rife with choices and opportunities of varying importance, and we often make decisions in haste, with the wrong information, or with the wrong mindset.

Of course hindsight is twenty-twenty. Decisions will always be made with incomplete information[1]. We will never know in advance how things will play out—what roles chance and fortune will take—and thus we make decisions on best guesses with the information at hand. How could we have known in college that the computer industry was a high-growth industry? That Yahoo stock would skyrocket? That this person was a better match for us than that one? When hindsight *is* twenty-twenty we cannot fault ourselves with picking something and running with it. As long as the decisions made were the best ones given the information available, we cannot, and never would really, fault ourselves for them.

However, at many other times, we made decisions with the wrong mindsets or perspectives and wound up regretting them. Instead of thinking about all the consequences and making decisions based on what was most desirable in the long term, we took shortcuts in thought and did what was expected or what was most comfortable at the time. We took jobs only for financial gain at extreme personal costs; or we rushed to have children because that was what was expected by family. Looking back, perhaps the sacrifice of youth was too high for those jobs, or perhaps having kids early-on was not worth the quality-of-life sacrifice. By having predetermined mindsets from the start we automatically filtered out information that contradicted with those original mindsets, which led to making decisions based not on the available information, but on the *comfortable* information.

Predetermined mindsets are ideas, notions, biases, and thought structures that form in the subconscious mind, and thus without us having overtly chosen them. They are the political

---

[1] The notion that people make educated decisions based on imperfect information is called "bounded rationality," implying that there are bounds to the amount of knowledge we can collect and know given any decision point. The economist Herbert Simon propounded this idea, stating that people always make decisions good enough to satisfy their needs and suffice the given situation, or "satisfice."

slantings, the racial prejudices, the instinctual drives, or the religious beliefs, for example, that are held close to our hearts. But as important as these mindsets become, they coalesce mostly in early childhood with minimal active or rational choice on our part, determined by childhood experiences and human nature. They become lodged in our minds early on as belief structures necessary to see and navigate through the world. These predetermined mindsets are indeed necessary in that they create the mental structures through which we see the world and put it into context; a context without which it would be impossible to process the abundant amount of sensory information that is constantly received. This context tells which information is important, and which is not, and why. But past pubescence, these mindsets become dated and need to be replaced with ones more pertinent to our lives and experiences, rather than those of our parents' or caveman ancestors'.

To not let go of childhood mindsets in search of our own is to repeat our parents' mistakes, to our own detriment. In keeping these predetermined mindsets we chain ourselves to the past and to our genetic shortcomings. Our quality of life suffers when we make decisions with predetermined mindsets because the structure that these mindsets impose on ourselves and our experiences do not necessarily fit or make sense. Although seeing these mental structures in ourselves is difficult, and rooting them out in search of new ones even more so, this book will empower the reader with the knowledge to do so, and in turn reclaim his moral and existential freedoms.

One shortcoming of these predetermined mindsets is the judgement of the experiences that result from our decisions. In other words, because we make decisions based on certain mindsets, we come to expect a set of results from those decisions that reflect our mindsets, and all ensuing experiences are internally judged or qualified based on those expectations. If we took a job only for financial gain, then we would measure the success of our careers solely in terms of money. This pre-qualification of our experiences based on predetermined mindsets is devastating for two reasons. First, it paints experiences under the guise of success and failure according to how well expectations are met, a guise that short-changes those experiences. What if we do not get the bonuses we expected because of economic conditions? To think that the past years spent on the job were thus consequently wasted would be devastating. All experiences are of some value, didactic or otherwise, and to box them into qualified successes or failures is to waste that value.

The second problem with qualifying experiences based on mindsets is the flip side of the first—it blinds us to the lighter characteristics and/or learnings of an experience if they do not lie within the realm of expectations. Literature is rife with romantic examples. In James Joyce's *Araby*, a tale of childhood romance, the protagonist apotheosizes his love interest to the point of constructing an imaginary temple for her—Araby. In the end, he is disappointed because he realizes reality cannot hope to meet his imagination. The same is true of F. Scott Fitzgerald's *Winter Dreams*, another tale of an impossible romance. The anticipation of Judy Jones, the protagonist's love interest, is so high, that when the protagonist returns, he loses interest in the real Judy Jones, because she does not and cannot meet expectations, again losing out on romance.

The shortcomings of predetermined mindsets are waste and harm, but without greater insight, acclimatization causes us to mistake them for being a natural part of life. Euphemistically, and tragically, they become tolerable. Ignorance is bliss, if the human condition is one of unwitting masochism. But far worse, and far better, is to have hindsight into the waste and harm these mindsets cause. Far worse is the feeling of regret that accompanies the acknowledgement of the waste and harm. We have all experienced that regret; the ball that sits at the pit of a man's stomach and grows with every realization of a poor decision using bad faith; a decision that lead to a missed opportunity or a deleterious outcome. It is the feeling the dehabilitated sixty-year-old feels when he realizes he should have been playing sports or having fun with his children on weekends when he had the chance, instead of being at the office. It is Charles Foster Kane in *Citizen Kane* longing for the childhood he never had, and missing the idealism he started out with, when on his deathbed he calls out for "Rosebud," his childhood sled. The things that should have happened in life did not, or the things that should not have happened did, solely because of bad judgement. That bad judgement sits squarely on the shoulders of the decision-maker and weighs him down with the full force of responsibility. We come to feel this way when we realize that we ourselves fabricated the structure imposed on our minds voluntarily and unknowingly; that we have incarcerated ourselves in our minds when every inch of our being cries out for freedom. No bars and locks at the office kept us there, the bars and locks existed only in our minds.

Regret makes predetermined mindsets painful, making them far worse by adding salt to injury. But regret can also make the situation far better when the pain becomes intolerable, inciting the person into action. The intolerable pain of regret opens up our eyes to our inherent freedom of self-invention. This freedom is the key to ensuring that the decisions we make in life, and the paths we choose to take, will not be made according to mindsets and structures of which we are unaware, and thus of which we will regret. Although it is reasonable and necessary to make decisions based on structures and mindsets, those mindsets need to be chosen rather than predetermined for full freedom of choice. The principles and ideals by which we live are forms of mindsets and structures, but as long as we have chosen to live by those principles instead of having developed them as biases, then we have not forfeited our freedom.

Transparency, Knowledge, and Freedom

The freedom explored in this book is to be understood under the context of precluding regret through transparent thought. I will discuss different forms of freedom and the different barriers to freedom to make those barriers transparent and transform life from habit to possibility, and attenuate or eliminate regret. Every barrier encountered and torn down is one less "should have" or "could have" that we have to face in the future because now we "can" and know that perhaps we "should," and will not regret. I will discuss our instinctual nature and the structure that it imposes on our behaviors to bring clarity to our motivations, allowing us the freedom to rise above our primal tendencies in seeking higher-order transcendence and fulfillment. I will discuss the workings of the mind to allow us to leverage those mental mechanisms to our advantage rather than be hindered by them. I will discuss the limitations of cultural knowledge and language to give us the ability to unveil more choices based on new viewpoints and new ways of thinking. In every case the intent is to first unearth all of the baggage that we carry around in the form of assumptions, then to learn to open that baggage by questioning all of those assumptions, and lastly finish by packing a new, smaller, more personal and comfortable bag to carry by picking and choosing the assumptions that are most reasonable to us. The three topics discussed here—the instincts, neurophilosophy, and culture—are at the base of our house-of-assumption-cards, toppling everything above them with their own fall.

The context for freedom is dichotomously opportunity and regret, the method is the Socratic ideal: the practical application of a philosophical notion through enlightened questioning. The more we question ourselves and our motives, and the more we get to know ourselves, the more enlightened and fulfilled we can become. Questioning yields the constant widening of our views and insights into the possibilities of life. As we unearth and break down our blind assumptions, we build and forge new, enlightened ones that focus us on those things that we deem most appropriate to ourselves and our experiences. As we vacate the blind-assumption house built by personal history and evolution, we inhabit the enlightened one we build ourselves.

This book consists of two main sections, each discussing a different type of assumption base or structural imposition on thought. One section pertains to the structures imposed by man's genetic nature, mostly discussions on instincts and the hardwiring of the human mind. The other pertains to the assumptions that are externally acquired or developed, mostly discussions about culture, language, and the behavioral softwiring of the human mind.

Those things that constitute the brain's hardwiring are the driving force behind how we learn, act, and think, and are universal. They need to be identified so that we can be aware of them and how they influence our lives and behaviors so that we are not prisoners to them. We are all bound by the fact that we are human, and understanding our intrinsic limitations will help us transcend them. It is essential for us to unlock how we inherently process and use our subject-dependent experiences to grow and change based on those unchangeable characteristics that make us human so we can use those processes for our own advantage, as opposed to our genes' advantage (more on this later.)

As opposed to our hardwired characteristics, those things that are softwired are personal to each one of us and thus vary from one individual to the next. Although based on experience, the assumptions and limitations that we develop over time become embedded in our subconscious minds and are beyond our ability to notice directly. In order to bring those assumptions to light and act despite them, we have to actively monitor and analyze our own behaviors and thoughts, subjects discussed in more detail in the second part of this book.

Our abilities to make enlightened decisions will preempt the regret that arises from not knowing we had choices. Knowledge allows us to fully bear our existential responsibilities so that the histories written on those universal stones are written *by* us, and not *for* us.

Part One:

The Importance of Freedom

Chapter 1.

The Importance of Freedom

The Meaning of Freedom

T he introduction to this book discussed the significance of freedom in terms of the repercussions of the knowledge and exercising of choices. It is the explicit knowledge of choices which impels us to make decisions to bring authenticity to life. What follows next is a discussion of what freedom ultimately means, and how its definition fits in with that meaning.

Ask anybody what "freedom" means and he will be hard pressed to come up with a definition that's neither merely illustrative nor metaphorical. What is this thing that is so dear to humanity, having waged wars and atrocities in its name? The difficulty in its definition stems from the seemingly infinite number of variations of the word based on the context and level of abstraction. Is it a principle, a state of being, an emotional sensation, a human abstraction, or a physical right? The meaning of freedom to a prisoner is not the same as it is to a revolutionary, which is yet different to a divorcé. In each case the context changes, which means that in each case the meaning of the word will also change. Without any of the definitions being more right than another, sizeable room for interpretation exists that enables us to find our own way of extracting the meaning.

When people first think of freedom, they usually think of its traditional definitions based upon political and religious contexts. Political freedoms are those that arise from man's ability to remove obstacles in order to achieve chosen goals. For example, if a law exists in a country that forbids certain people from voting, then the removal of that law can be considered a political freedom. The obstacle is the law, and the goal is that of being able to vote. The U.S. is an example of a country with a wide range of political freedoms and civil liberties, where its citizens are generally immune from arbitrary exercises of authority, including enslavement, detention, and oppression. These are all based on the political premise that a man should be able to achieve chosen goals with as few obstacles as possible.

Religious freedoms are also traditional in context. These pertain to the ability to attain self-realization in the eyes of our gods, as well the antithetical exercise of free will. The former refers to our rights and abilities to fulfill the role and existence that our gods have created and have meant for us to enact. For example, the Catholic pope would probably state that God put him on earth to become pope and spread the word of Jesus. Anything that would preclude him from becoming such and doing so would be an obstruction of his religious freedom of self-realization. To borrow a Shakespearean metaphor, God, being omniscient, knows the universe's script, including all the parts played by all its actors. Every human that ever existed has a role to play according to this universal script, and the ability of each human to play out his or her role is considered to be a freedom of self-realization.

The flip side is the belief in free will, or our ability to fulfill our own goals and our own versions of existence free from predeterministic forces. This scenario does not include a universal script since existence is chaotic and interdependent, making any type of prognostication by a divine being impossible. In other words, nature interacts in such a complex way that it is impossible to predict, even for an all-knowing being. The basis of free will here lies in our ability to choose despite historical and external influences, whether those influences are divine or Cartesian reductionist. By Cartesian reductionism I am referring to the now defunct belief, credited to Rene Descarte, that a mind powerful enough to capture the state of the universe at a point in time could theoretically prognosticate the future by playing out all the future interactions of all the particles according to the laws of science. Belief in free will assumes that the future is wholly unpredictable and independent of the past, and as humans we are free to choose with the full force of this independence.

Cartesian reductionism rose in popularity thanks to Isaac Newton and his laws of science. In Newton's time people were able to predict the future paths and locations of objects according to Newtonian mathematics. Throw a ball at a certain angle with a certain force, and we could predict where and when it will land. Reductionism figures that the atomic world was only a miniature version of our world, and thus just as predictable. Instead of only one ball, a near infinite number of balls existed, each with a location and an applied force. Get someone or something smart enough, and he could trace the paths of all the atomic balls, and thus map the future, since everything in the universe was made of atoms. Instead of self-realization in the eyes of God, we had self-realization in the eyes of science. This originated with Descarte's reductionist philosophies, and then flourished with the popularization of Newtonian physics. Science was the new god that ruled the universe. That is until the advent of quantum physics pushed it off its perch.

Besides the traditional ones, many other philosophical freedoms exist. For example, existentialists posit that freedom is the need for, and existence of, obstacles. This is in stark contrast to the traditional definitions that require the absence of obstacles. According to existentialist theory, freedom is pointless without

obstacles. Just like light defines darkness, obstacles define freedom. For example, if no laws prohibited voting, then we would
all be voters. The idea of being free to vote loses its meaning
when everyone can vote. It's akin to everyone being human. Strangers would call us nuts if we went around proclaiming our happiness of being free to be human. They would say that there is no
such thing as being free to be human, we just simply are human.
We cannot *not* be human. Just as if everyone could vote, no such
thing as being free to vote would exist. Freedom only comes into
existence when there are obstacles. Existentialists desire not to
get rid of obstacles (assuming reasonable obstacles, of course),
but instead to focus on overcoming them. The difference is subtle,
but significant.

The second type of existential freedom is that of self-invention. This will be discussed in more detail later, but basically it is
the self granted freedom to choose to behave in any desired way,
irrespective of personal history, culture, expectations, physical
makeup, or any other worldly influences. It goes hand-in-hand
with moral freedom—the freedom to choose our own moral
and ethical codes and structures irrespective of worldly influences.

A whole book could be written just on the definitions of
freedom, but that is not my intent here. I've listed a few definitions to impart the significance as it relates to philosophy. Although the definitions are wholly subjective, depending on our
personal systems of beliefs, the meanings are not. Freedom is the
yardstick by which we measure our abilities to attain self-fulfillment. The freer we are, whatever that means to us, the more we
can become self-fulfilled, and the less suffering and frustration.
Thus, the ultimate meaning of freedom is self-fulfillment, while
the definition that is personally chosen determines the manner
by which we can achieve it. We can become self-fulfilled either
through self-realization, free will, the removal of obstacles, the
overcoming of obstacles, or whatever other definition of freedom we embrace. The point is not that trying to come up with a

THE IMPORTANCE OF FREEDOM

definition is useless because it is murky and arguable, but that it is wholly significant exactly because it is subjective and defining as a personal principle. Tell me your definition and you are also implicitly telling me what value life and its experiences hold for you.

The Burden of Freedom

That we fight and work so hard to win and preserve our physical, political, and religious freedoms is ironic, when every day we willingly give up our moral and existential ones. It is easier to lose these latter freedoms because the chains and jails that incarcerate them are symbolic and psychological rather than physical, and are built slowly over time. We cannot see or touch a bias, and it is not wrapped around our ankles in a matter of minutes. It is easier to fight an enemy, or work for a reward, that we can see, hear, touch, and smell. However, this does not tell the whole story, because if these freedoms were important enough, or easy enough, we would not let them slip away. But we do. We all have our ingrained habits, our unexplainable yet comfortable routines, our biases, and a touch of stubbornness to boot.

Attaining and maintaining our moral and existential freedoms requires work and painful self honesty. These goals, along with the power of choice, come with caveats. They entail the assuming of responsibility, which can be frightening or incapacitating. In a sense, freedom can be its own worst enemy. Complete freedom (if the concept can even exist) is a difficult and oppressive quality to endure, regardless of the type or form. This dilemma is known by existentialist philosophers as the "anguish of freedom[2]."

We anguish over the burden of choices, given that a mesh of work, risk, and uncertainty is involved in any decision. The multifaceted burden of freedom begins with the possibility of infi-

---

[2] Olson, pgs. 51-63

nite options. In order to completely eliminate the uncertainty within choice, we would have to first list the infinite relevant number of variables, possible circumstances, and viable possibilities. Even if the choice is binary, infinite gradations of variables and circumstances exist. Another "what if . . ." question can always be thrown into the puzzle. Obviously, though, we never possess an infinite amount of time to think of all the "what ifs" and list all of the combinations of variables and circumstances, as well as options, in any decision. We must, as a natural fact of life, always generalize, aggregate, and assume away most of the factors and options in any decision to be able to act. The more trivial the decision, the more it is assumed away. For instance, every time we talk to a stranger as part of the normal workings of life, we usually assume that he speaks English and shares enough of our experience of culture to understand the context and content of our words. Our choices in these circumstances are the language and manner in which to talk to these strangers. We do not first ask them if they speak English, and we do not probe to understand their cultural understanding of each of our words in order to adjust our conversation. In most circumstances to do so would be a waste of time as well as an annoyance, so we make certain sets of assumptions about the people that we meet on a day-to-day basis.

The end result of assuming away most of the decision-making factors is a quicker and more efficient decision-making process, but along with that also comes a large amount of uncertainty. Important information might have been lost in the process that would have led to a more effective decision. By assuming that someone shares our same cultural background, we also assume they understand our words in the same way, risking offending or embarrassing them, or with the additional risk of misunderstanding each other altogether without even knowing it. We create uncertainty by cutting corners and in turn create an accompanying risk of making the wrong decisions. This risk carries along with it a burden of stress, or preemptively, anguish, in varying degrees depending upon the significance of the decision at hand.

Given that we always have to create decision-making short cuts, and thus always create uncertainty, we will feel more anguish with increasing awareness or cognizance of freedom. Life would be less burdensome if we were neither allowed to make decisions, nor given many choices. Instead, the more freedom we have, the more decisions we can make, and the more choices we are given, the more uncertainty that exists, and the more anguish we feel. A trade-off arises between work and uncertainty in the face of a decision, but in either case there is anguish.

Thus we create shortcuts and are lazy in order to be efficient with our time. But we also decrease our freedoms in order to reduce the amount of anguish we feel. In view of our inherent propensities towards laziness, it takes confidence, energy, and providence to go through the larger set of decision-making steps that freedom allows, as well as to increase freedoms in general. To search the mind's recesses to gather a list of viable possibilities at a decision point is not easy, and it is even more difficult to garner the important set of criteria upon which to measure the possibilities. In fact to always do so becomes impossible, thus sometimes making assumptions and going on gut-feel more rational for time and sanity's sake. However, by and large it is just easier to fall into the lazy route of always following the most blatant choice to circumvent an intelligent decision-making process. With walls, boundaries, blindspots, and limitations, freedoms can also be reduced to a few or none, making the decision process attractively clean and simple.

But the most onerous burden of freedom is its accountability and responsibility. Although following through with the decision-making process takes mental energy, following through based solely on one's judgment takes courage. When all consequences and results lie on the shoulders of a person and his decision, the courage to act becomes daunting, especially when those consequences are long-lasting.

It is far easier to flee from responsibility and decisions by living according to the expectations of parents, friends, priests, and society in general. We all are drawn toward mass opinion. Little risk is involved in following the path that others have followed and have set for us. Personally, and to others, we can justify our decision as simply following a precedent with little risk of responsibility. When following others' examples and expectations, responsibility is shared with them since they were partially involved in the original decision-making process.

For example, in the movie *Twelve Angry Men*, Henry Fonda's character, Mr. Davis, has to work hard to change the verdict of any one juror after they have all voted guilty because for the juror it entails i) going against the opinion of the majority, and ii) having to make the effort to see things in a new light, versus staying with what is comfortable. Once a guilty verdict gained momentum as the jurors voted successively, each additional juror was then further entrenched into voting likewise because of the difficulty of arguing against large odds and the ease of deferment of judgement and responsibility to the majority. It took a courageous and free-thinking Mr. Davis to first vote differently, and then to take the time, effort, and energy to sway they group's opinion. Mr. Davis' risk is that if it turns out that the defendant is guilty, Mr. Davis will have to bear accusations, finger pointing, and social reprisals from having stood out on his own and swayed the group, not to mention the ridicule and abuse he took from the jurors during the period of deliberation.

Consequences are fully borne when no outside influence helps make the decision, thus making it riskier and demanding more courage. No one exists at whom to point a finger but ourselves, no one with whom to share the shame or blame. This means that we must fully bear the burden of accountability, and the work or pain from reprisal of responsibility, over a decision that fails.

On the other hand, if we follow mass opinion we manage to spread accountability and responsibility over so many people that the resulting amount hoisted on the individual is infinitesimal. The allure of the posse is strong. If the posse kills an innocent man, it can divide the blame umpteen ways, and the individual can hide behind the mass of people. If a vigilante kills an innocent man, he solely bears the weight of responsibility and the ensuing consequences.

Building walls and boundaries to comfortably limit freedom takes on many forms, from simply following mass opinion, the expectations heaped on by parents, society, and peers, religious moral and social doctrines, to adopting rigid philosophical codes. However, it would be unduly short sighted and judgmental to say that building walls such as following religious doctrine is deleterious to well being. In the end, the only true judge is the person himself for he alone knows the basis upon which he will feel fulfilled. Some limits and walls must be built in order for a person to function properly in life. No authority exists regarding what is a good boundary and what is a bad one, save the individual's.

An important tenet of this book that forms one of the foundations of responsible freedom is that to choose to not be free is still to choose, as long as the choice is done in full cognizance. To build that wall, to believe in this religion, to define oneself as something, are all authentic[3] actions if we are aware of them. If we choose to confine ourselves to our houses by locking ourselves in, in other words to *not* be mobile, then our being is authentic because we used our freedom to choose to be physically bound. The purpose of this book is thus not to make noncommittal wafflers out of its readers, but instead to reinstate the responsibility of freedom.

A second foundational tenet is that to *not* choose is *to* choose, which implies cognizance of the ability to choose, which im-

---

[3] The notion of authenticity is an existentialist one derived from the notion of creating one's self in full cognizance of the self. In other words, a person is authentic when his life is defined by himself through the choices he makes freely, rather than when happening by chance and circumstance. If this is not clear now, it will become clear in the following chapters.

plies authenticity. For example, to be agnostic—to neither choose to believe nor to not believe in the existence of divine beings—is both authentic and responsible. On the other hand, to not be aware of a choice is inauthentic. To not choose to be agnostic, atheistic, or religious is inauthentic as far as the decision-maker is unaware of the choice, where to not choose means that the person is none of those things, or that he fell into one of them without thinking. In the end we are all inauthentic to some degree since we can never be aware of all the choices we have. However, it is a far worse crime of authenticity to fall into something than to be completely oblivious to it all. Some inauthenticity is fine, though, since we were never meant to be perfect, but instead could strive for perfection.

Freedom and Society

A second caveat to freedom needs to be considered as we choose our paths in life. The first caveat, the burden of freedom, balanced the benefits of moral and existential freedoms with some disadvantages according to our characters. There is beauty in the simplicity and ease of moving within the boundaries of moral and intellectual dogma. When choices are predetermined, leading to quick and painless decisions, life becomes like a feather that is moved by the winds and breezes of circumstance. Burden-reducing benefits exist from following a narrow path, and those benefits are rightfully enticing. Simple bliss is a wholly justifiable aim (purporting that there should be more to it all is indefensible outside the realm of personal philosophy.) We can choose to be hedonistic, and no one else would have either the right nor power to change that. As far as a path that is taken by us affects us alone, that path is fully justifiable in our and everyone else's eyes. To impose a definition of fulfillment upon others, and therefore impose a philosophical or moral doctrine upon them, is impossible.

The second caveat to freedom is that it cannot be considered in individual isolation since no man is an island and any choice we make will affect those around us. Inasmuch as this is true, a basis exists upon which the imposition of standard, communal protocols is justifiable. Complete freedom makes no sense on an individual basis due to the waste and inefficiency of it, as was previously discussed, and complete freedom makes no sense in a social setting either, due to the effects of an individual's actions on those around him. However, these confines to freedom are limited to the effects of social interaction. The impetus of the interaction that we have with our surrounding society is our personal philosophy, and as such that philosophy is solely within the bounds of our judgment. If, for example, hedonistic simplicity and happiness yields us fulfillment, it is our right to choose a path that follows that philosophy. If our paths clash with accepted social protocols, it is the right of the society to reprisal. But it was also our right to choose that path to begin.

Mature societies often mistake governmental authority as a natural right rather than a given one. It is no one's and no group's naturally given, a priori right to have any kind of authority over any other person or group. That authority can only be granted or given willfully. Thus, governments have no naturally given right to executive authority, and religious institutions have no naturally given right to moral authority. They are merely granted that right by all the encompassing individuals. But once we agree to live within a given society, we implicitly agree to grant the governing institutions certain authorities, and the governing authority is then obliged to enforce that authority—we have entered into Rousseau's "Social Contract[4]." The individual is still

---

[4] According to Rousseau "… the social order is a sacred right which serves as a basis for all rights. And as it is not a natural right, it must be one founded on covenants… since each man gives himself to all, he gives himself to no one; and since there is no associate over whom he does not gain the same rights as others gain over him, each man recovers the equivalent of everything he loses, and in the bargain he acquires more power to preserve what he has."

free to act and live as he wishes, but society has the right to enforce its implicit agreement with the individual. The individual does not *have* to live in any given manner, but he does have to live with the consequences of his actions, and therefore must weigh them when making choices.

The physical impingement of laws on freedom is obvious— break the law and be fined or go to jail. But what is not so obvious is the moral impingement they might have on freedom. Again, moral freedom is acting based on circumstances and consequences rather than just dogma. However, we oftentimes fall into the trap of ruling out actions simply because they go against societal law. "I'm not going to do that because it is against the law" is not an uncommon argument. We accept and we live by the fact that laws limit our physical freedoms, but the point is we should not allow them to limit our moral freedoms unknowingly.

Sometimes laws go against our principles, or sometimes the gain of rebelling is worth the detriments and the risks involved. The American Revolution, and the American Constitution, especially the amendment allowing individuals to bear arms, are based on the notion that laws can go counter to the majority's moral principles and that individuals need to heed this. A contemporary example, besides obvious ones such as Jim Crow laws, is the speed trap. We have all had the misfortune of going through speed traps, highway zones with ridiculously low speed limits placed in the hope of increasing government revenue through the issuing of tickets. In this scenario, breaking the law and safely going faster than the speed limit to save otherwise wasted minutes or hours is rational. Most people have exceeded the speed limit at one time or another in similar scenarios because they rationally decided that the gain in travel time was worth the risk of the ticket and the effect on society. This is a rational decision, and probably one that in the end does gain more than it loses, assuming the person is rational and driving with proper care and control. The person, and society as a whole, gains productive

THE IMPORTANCE OF FREEDOM

time at the low risk of a ticket, and negligible risk in personal and societal security. The law in this case is an irrational tax on productivity.

Losing sight of the fact that laws exist for the net gain to society is easy, but for the sake of fairness laws are also blind. This does not mean that people should obey them blindly, though. They don't always guarantee a net gain, or relative justice, and therefore should be followed mindfully and rationally, not blindly. We give up physical freedoms for the sake of a net gain to society, and thus a net gain to us, but we do not have to give up our moral freedoms, too.

Inauthenticity of being arises when an individual mistakes the implicit social contract as a concrete structure for behavior rather than an agreed-upon definition of responsibility. The problem of authenticity occurs when we live according to an external authority, or live by the contract "guidelines," without thinking or knowing of alternatives. There is honor in choosing a life of bliss from ignorance of alternatives when that path is indeed chosen; we can choose not to know something, but then we are not completely ignorant since we know we do not know. Stupidity arises when we *fall* into a path. The dilemma is that the walls of moral and philosophical incarceration from social structures are often built before we have harnessed the ability of critical thought. Religion, political credos, prejudices, and biases are all inculcated in childhood so that by adolescence, when man has gained the ability of critical thought, the walls have hardened. It is no coincidence that most people have the same political stances and religious beliefs as their parents, even though countless options exist. It takes foresight and intellectual courage to implode the walls built through childhood education, but to not do so is to be condemned to a life, rather than be given the gift of one. Walls and boundaries have their benefits, but those benefits are only conferred when the walls and boundaries are personally chosen and built, rather than externally forged.

Having walls and boundaries does not necessarily imply ignorance or closed-mindedness. We all have walls that we've built out of necessity. They lend structure to thought, and allow for swift decisions. To not build some walls and boundaries is to be condemned to mental paralysis. Structure in thought is necessary, and bounding options is an important processing step in analysis. But again, thought can be considered enlightened only if we are cognizant of the walls and boundaries that give us structure to think. By not knowing this structure of thought and action we are relegating ourselves to the role of a lab rat following the scent of cheese in a maze. How much easier for the rat to get to the cheese if he could create his own maze, or get rid of it altogether!

The Role of Language

Many of the walls, boundaries, and frustrations that are inculcated into man are derived from language and the structure it places on thought and communication. Because language is a tool of communication, it creates a paradigm for thought and action. Our ability to conceive of ideas and plans of action are both enabled and limited by our ability to use words to communicate these ideas and plans of actions to ourselves and to others. Similar to language, steel beams and concrete are tools that enable the construction of buildings, but because of their properties, they limit the types of buildings that can be built by them. We cannot build a log cabin using steel beams and concrete, just like we cannot speak French without knowledge of French words and grammar. However, the main problem with language is not its limitation as a tool of communication. We can only use the tools we are given and that we learn. To escape the confines of our tools, we can learn and acquire more, but then we are still limited to this larger set of tools. If we wanted to build log cabins but only possessed steel beams and concrete, we would have to acquire logs. By acquiring logs we have expanded our scope of

tools and types of buildings that can be built, but are still limited
in that we cannot build glass or bamboo buildings, or mud huts.
We will always be limited, no matter how much we acquire and
learn.

The real confinement by language is our habit of confusing
symbols and models with the real thing. Words are not the things-
in-themselves, but mere symbols and models of those things. The
word "man" is not man, but a string of letters symbolic of man.
The word "fairness" does not describe a concept found in nature, but is instead a model of behavior. In its original derivation, the word meant to describe man's need to create balance
and to force fairness on the environment because of his internal
behavioral tendencies: to ensure personal survival against cheat-
ing and encroachment, we have developed a psychological scale
against which things are weighed and balanced,[5] a way to ensure that we're not being robbed and not creating unnecessary
enemies. Society flourishes only when we give and receive in
roughly equal measures, and thus we have developed this built-
in mental scale, whether through genetic or social evolution.
But now we have taken this internal system of tracking favors
and debts and misapplied it to the external world. This psychological balance, extended to society and nature, has been given
a name: fairness. Fairness and justice do not exist in nature; the
sun and moon set and rise without justification. But in extending
it to the world, we have created stress for ourselves because it
does not exist in kind. We use fairness and justice as means to
explain phenomena without directly attributable causes, and to
come to terms with life's uncontrollable variables. One event
otherwise independent from another can be given reason through
senses of fairness and justice. For example, it seems "unfair" to
be born only to die, to suffer without reason. But the problem is
not with the unfairness of life or the suffering inherent to it, but
with our confusion with the difference between fairness as a natural
concept and as a model. We find no attributable cause or reason for the formation and destruction of life, for the suffering

---

[5] Aronson, pg. 391-3

inherent to it; but through a sense of fairness we can give suffering meaning by imputing that the suffering was caused in expiation of some previously perpetrated sin.

The concept of fairness in its original derivation merely models a human psychological phenomenon, but the word now has been confused as being a real thing, more than a model, extended it to fit our desire to find causation in all phenomena. The repercussions of this extension are far reaching. Remove the concept of fairness from within us, and we remove our discomfort with the capriciousness of nature, but we also create discomfort with our own non-capricious behavior. This concept of fairness has lead to the creation of even more concepts to ameliorate the discomfort caused by the extension of original derivation, concepts both rational and irrational.

Although fairness is only one example, society and language are rife with cases of misapplication of concepts. These misapplications cause great psychological dissonance and frustrations as life fails to match our ideas of it. As we expect and plan for something dependent on our views of the workings of the world, frustration arises when our expectations and plans are not met. Time and energy are lost in bad planning and bad decisions. The roles that our views and expectations play in guiding choices impact our freedom. Misuse of language can lead to a blindness of choices and the making of bad decisions. As Voltaire's *Candide* learned the hard way, things do not always turn out for the better, nor do a higher justice or fairness in life necessarily exist.

To regain sensibility in expectations and thought, William James' pragmatic and David Hume's empirical philosophies are good yardsticks and paradigms. If an idea, theory, or concept is not derived from (Hume) nor impacts (James) practical life, it should not apply. The concept of fairness is derived from the human tendency towards psychological scorekeeping, thus is derived from practical life, and does apply to those related circumstances where an individual gives or is due something. In this use fairness is practical in its application since it is empirically derived and applied. However, when it is applied to things

THE IMPORTANCE OF FREEDOM

that cannot and do not keep score, such as nature, then it is no longer practicable since it is neither derived nor applied in empirical means. In other words, observations of nature[6] did not lead to the conception of fairness since it is not imbedded in nature's structures or laws, and cannot be applied pragmatically since the concept has no impact outside of human imagination. No matter how much it rains today, or how much I pray, or how much I sacrifice, nature does not owe me a bright, sunny day tomorrow, even if I think it fair. The sun and clouds do not know the concept of fairness, and cannot apply it, no matter how much I want them to. Freedom lies in my ability to think and communicate using language as my tool, without creating the blind spots and false expectations from the misapplication of that tool.

The Derivation of Value

Earlier I described the anguish inherent in freedom being derived from the consequences of its use upon unique and irreversible lives. I also talked about freedom having meaning as it relates to a person's ability to seek self-fulfillment. Basically, both these points assumed that life held some kind of inherent meaning or value—the cause of the anguish and the force for self-fulfillment. Anguish arises when value is left untapped, and self-fulfillment arises from feeling valuable. Our abilities to create value through our decisions and actions lend importance to freedom as we make the implied choices. Freedom matters when its practice and implementation matter; i.e., when one option or choice creates more value than another, and when that choice adds to a life-long chain. But what is still missing is why a single life, and thus any and all choices within it, should have any value to begin with, why the assumption was made.

It is true that life is pointless, but pointless within the larger scheme of things. The sun does not care about us, and our lives

---

[6] Some people might argue that there are other animals besides man that keep mental tabs, but I'm using nature in this argument to stand for inanimate nature, the nature that physics describes.

are irrelevant to it. In the smaller scheme of things, however, in the scheme that encompasses us and our friends and family, our lives and everything within them have a point. Happiness, fulfillment, and love are great reasons to do things, and great reasons for living. And we all do, by and large, lead our lives as if they mattered, fretting over decisions and consequences, working hard to meet objectives, fearing our impending deaths. We do place a great deal of value and meaning to our own lives, and to the lives of the people around us. We feel anguish, we fight wars in the name of freedom, and we work tirelessly to fulfill our dreams and goals. As we all have lived in a manner similar to this, we all have also at one point or another stopped and wondered why.

In essence, life is precious because it is finite. Economists say that the primary basis of value of any object is its scarcity. The less there is of something in relation to its demand, the more valuable it becomes. Diamonds, for example, are not valuable necessarily because they are beautiful or useful. Diamonds are valuable because of an (artificial) shortage of the gems, and thus a scarcity. The coal from which diamonds are created, on the other hand, is so freely mined and traded, that there is an abundance rather than a scarcity, and is thus less valuable.

Of all the things known to any one of us, life is the scarcest, and thus the most precious. Non-renewable, it is relatively short in duration, completely unique, and interdependent with all other things. In this context life's value is so obvious that it almost seems like a self-referencing, and thus nullifying, proposition. Life is valuable because life is scarce. This would not be so obvious if we had immortals walking among us, though. Life as we know it is finite, but it need not be necessarily so. There could be gods or alien races that are immortal, meaning that the scarcity of a life's time is not a necessary property. In other words, living beings need not necessarily be mortal to be alive, which means that the duration of a life is an extrinsic property.

If I lived during the middle ages and had a life expectancy of thirty years, while someone else lived in modern times and had an expectancy of seventy years, and yet someone else is immortal, we each will place different values on each second of our lives, and thus different values on life. For an immortal, time would have no value since every second would be replaceable. But being mortal, we do not possess an infinite amount of time. Every second counts, and thus our need to extract as much value from each one as possible. Freedom's paramount importance comes from this need to extract value, for if we are not free to do what we wish with our time, we could possibly be wasting it. As valuable as time is, any waste comes at a high, and painful, price.

The inherent economic value of time is derived according to a number of factors, similar to how we value gifts. Every second of life, like a gift, is received and not requested, and is temporal and evanescent. Any gift is most valuable again, when scarce, and when used in all kinds of manners that are most impacting to the person. These gifts fulfill their owners the most.

Those moments in time, like trick gifts, that amuse and make us momentarily happy, are useful, but are the most fleeting. A smile or a laugh that is derived from something by its nature is spontaneous and fades as fast as it arises. Once heard, a joke loses its humor, and if overplayed, a game loses its charm. Happiness cannot be given, just like it cannot be sought. The result of the moment, the result of the gift, or the result of the search, will be a quickly fading smile or laugh. Happiness only lasts when it is an intrinsic state of being, or an emergent result of feeling fulfilled, and not as the result of an event or singular experience. A search for happiness is an unending search for those singular experiences that yield a moment's pleasure. We who embark on this search still harbor an emptiness derived from need or desire and do not have the luxury of lasting happiness. We will always be distracted both by that something that burns inside of us, and by the search itself. The two states of being—emptiness and momentary happiness—are at odds and cannot exist concomitantly for long. Life's desires must first be fulfilled in order for happiness to set in.

As far as gifts go, time is special because it is open-ended and completely malleable. Time is the gift of clay that we can mold into whatever shape suits us. We can mold it into a masterpiece of art, or into a gift to give to others, or into a useful tool for everybody, or we can turn it into a fun game such as Play-do. Its use is but a feat of the imagination, as long as we allow ourselves the freedom to imagine.

Eventually, though, the piece of clay will have to return to the mud and the earth from whence it came. But during the time it is still malleable, and even after its time has passed and it has hardened, that piece of clay takes on value not only for its owner, but for everybody else that comes into contact with it. This value is a function of three things and how those three things impact its owner: i) the clay's utility to all the people of any importance to the owner, including the owner himself; ii) the dependent nature of that utility[7] by the people that use the clay; and iii) the interdependent nature of that utility with past events. The utility is derived from the breadth and depth of use that the relevant people have for that clay, while importance is derived from how dependent the relevant people become to the use of the clay.

To step out of the metaphor, a chosen event or action is valuable as far as that event has breadth, or in other words is exciting or interesting because it is different either for the person himself or those around him. Time and energy have inherent value because of their scarcity. The more scarce the spent time and energy, the more valuable they become. Similar events and actions are less valuable by the fact that they are more numerous, or less scarce. Thus, the broader the events in our lives, the more valuable each one becomes, and thus the more valuable they become in their aggregation, which is what life is itself—the total sum of all events.

An event or action is also valuable as far as it has depth, or is

---

[7] Some people would object to the placement of value being dependent on human kind only. Is not the work and life of a caretaker of 1,000 dogs valuable to those dogs, regardless of the value he holds for humans? Perhaps, but in order to not get bogged down with this issue, in this book I will only discuss the type of value that can be assigned. As far as I can tell animals have no concept of value, and therefore cannot assign it.

but a link in a long chain of interdependent events or actions. Value is derived from interdependence because of the compounding of vested time and energy. As long as any one event in a chain of events depends upon those before and after it, then those events are interdependent, and the value of those events as a whole is greater than the sum of all the single events. Compounding comes from the fact that if events are interdependent, then value is derived not just from the sum of all of the events, but also from the manner in which they affect each other. If three events are sequentially interdependent, then the third yields value from the event itself, its relationship to the second event, and the second event's relationship with the first. A skilled billiards player derives value and enjoyment every time he plays, but his level of enjoyment goes up as his skills improve (an improvement which comes from previous playing experiences and which build upon each other). The compounding effect is great enough to question the rationale behind living merely a hedonistic life that is rife in breadth of experience, but dearth in depth.

The third factor in creating value is the dependence of others on an event or sequence of events in a subject's life. The more other people's time and energy is dependent on the actions or events of a subject, the more value they attribute to those actions and events, and thus the more they transfer to the person. Although I will take the subject of deriving value from others into more depth in later chapters, for now I will introduce the subject that it can be derived not only from the spending of our own time and energy, but also from that of others.

Although the perception of value is a wholly personal phenomenon, that perception can be altered and augmented by others. Value is derived from the utility others derive from us and their dependence on us through the transference of that value to us. That transference could be an acknowledging sentence, to a mere smile, to the general expression of an emotion such as love or envy. When someone smiles at us, he is acknowledging us, and he is acknowledging that we have impacted some of his valuable time in some way, thus transferring to us. That impact need not be positive for him as long as the transfer is perceived as positive by us (think of acts of vengeance). For it to be felt and counted personally, the value must be transferred. For example, in the 1946 movie *It's a Wonderful Life*, George Bailey (Jimmy Stewart's character) intends to commit suicide because he believes, in a moment of desperation, that his family and friends would be better off with his death. The police are after him, the bank examiner wants to close him down, and his family is broke. All these problems would go away with his death, plus everyone would get to collect on his insurance. However, George changes his mind and instead becomes elated when he realizes, with the help of his guardian angel, that his life has deeply impacted everyone around him, and will continue to do so. His actions have saved multitudes of lives, as well as influencing the growth and development of the town and its people through his involvement with the town bank. George became so engrossed in temporal problems that he failed to perceive his impact on the town and his family, leaving him empty. Only when he perceives and feels the transference of value by viewing what his town would have been like without him does George feel satisfied with the path he took. The town's collection of money in his honor is a graphic symbol of that value and its transference, reinforcing George's realization and feeling of fulfillment.

Free to use our imaginations, we execute on those things that yield us the most value. We can choose to have breadth of experiences, or depth (where we want depth, and to what degree), and how to interact with people to influence our level of interdependence with them. Though free to make all these choices, we must first acknowledge this freedom, and then act upon it. As easy as this sounds, it is in fact the most difficult task we face in our lives. We are constantly trying to limit our own freedoms to escape the inherent burdens.

Superficially we all want to be happy, but at a deeper level we all want to be fulfilled. Our personal definition of value is what defines how we reach fulfillment. We will feel fulfilled when we are on the right search for value and when that search becomes validated through the derivation of value. The individual's actions should strive towards reaching the goals and filling the aspirations that lie on that search for value, but he must first be free to undertake the search and execute on it.

Desire: the Human Itch

Freedom entails responsibility; not just the responsibility of the consequences of our actions, but also the responsibility to use that freedom wisely. Fleeting and comfortable happiness is a seductive temptress that tries to get us to take the easy way toward deriving value from our time, but we have seen that much more can be derived from breadth and depth of experience. As much as we all want to be happy and as much emphasis as society puts on happiness, it is a losing proposition. As Csikszentmihalyi notes, the human ego naturally tends toward a general state of misery, focusing on negative probabilities for the sake of contingency planning, and focusing on negative traits for the sake of betterment. As animals we are better suited for survival if we semi-neurotically focus on what things are wrong and what might go wrong. We basically live with an "itch," as Schopenhauer coined it, to better ourselves and our environment. Our neurosis creates that by first focusing on the negatives, and then creating the desire, need, or itch to improve upon them. As soon as that itch is scratched and our desires have been fulfilled, we feel a slight exhilaration or sense of happiness as a reward, only to then start the cycle over again by falling back into our neurosis[8].

---

[8] Csikszentmihalyi explains "There is no natural limit to desire. An unemployed person may think that if he made an income of thirty thousand a year he would be happy. But the person who does earn that sum thinks that if he could only make sixty thousand he would be happy... Many studies have shown that escalating expectations are the rule in every society where there is a possibility of improving one's lot."

The state of neurosis, along with the state of desire, is far longer in duration than the state of happiness. Coupled with the pain of work that may be involved, many philosophers label the natural human state as one of misery. Given the evanescent properties of happiness, we can understand why focusing on it is so futile. Focusing on happiness is also clearly not in our interest given the amount of work and desiring involved.

As existentialists put it, human nature involves constantly projecting the self and its state of affairs into a better state. Our nature is thus to be unhappy with our current selves to imagine a brighter future, and then to strive towards it. We seek to annihilate, or destroy, our current selves in order to get as far away from the nothingness from which we were originally born and to which we will return. In other words, we are constantly fighting to be and feel alive to spite our deaths.

We therefore do not strive to better ourselves because we feel misery, but instead feel misery because we seek to better ourselves. We suffer from an inherent miserable state of affairs, and that perpetual state is the gap between the projected self and the current self, from that which could be and that which is. It is our perpetual "itch." For example, the poor in the U.S. are levels of magnitude richer than the poor in China, yet we will find that on average U.S. suicide, criminal, and depression rates among the poor are much higher. Being poor is not necessarily miserable; in fact stoics, monks, and priests would rather be poor in order to seek a simpler life. Rather, being poor among rich, or being an "educated" poor, brings about greater desire and concomitant suffering. When a poor man can see or read about a better world he can imagine one, and then of course want it. This is not to say that the poor in China do not also suffer from the human itch, but it is less severe in light of their environment.

On the other hand we are kidding ourselves if we think we can change our internal programming and stop our neurotic, desirous nature. We can stop wanting about as much as we can stop breathing. We might be able to curb it, as monks are purported to do, but we cannot stop it. What we can do is derive utility, happiness, and fulfillment from work and desire themselves, rather than just their results. Instead of waiting to be happy from the attainment of something, we can derive pleasure from the mere fascination of wanting. This is the "stop and smell the roses" cliché. For example, we might see a painting, like it, and want it. We could focus on the fact of not having it and be miserable, or simply enjoy wanting it by admiring the characteristics that make us want to have it. The painting must be beautiful in some sense in order for us to want it, and therefore we should be able to get some satisfaction out of just admiring it. Instead of stopping to smell the roses, this is stopping to admire the paintings.

Similarly, instead of working toward a goal, and therefore being miserable because of the work we have to do, we could work for the sake of working and be fulfilled by it. In our example of the painting, if we no longer concentrate on having to have the painting, we no longer have to work to acquire it. This does not mean we should not have goals; in fact, we should *always* have them. The point being that the work we do to achieve goals should not be undertaken only for their sake, but also work's own sake. It is not bad to want a painting and work to obtain it. But given the value of time, why sacrifice a certain portion of it to make another portion better, if the sacrifice is not necessary? Sacrifice makes us prisoners of our own goals.

Freedom is derived from the ability to want without having-to-have, from working for work's sake instead of working for something, from man's ability to project himself into the future out of choice rather than out of merely being. To existentialists, the human condition entails consciously using freedom toward living a life of intensity, and ultimately fulfillment. It is about submerging one's subjective self within the midst of the world to manipulate it and be manipulated by it, rather than being an objectivized stone to be thrust by the currents. This manipulation of the world involves an understanding of the self and its

environment, as well as the attainment of freedom to do so. If
one is merely a victim of instincts and circumstances, then one
has not used his freedom to live, and has instead become an
object in the world, rather than a subject in the midst of the
world.

Part Two:

Internal Currents

Chapter 2.

The Strings that Bind

Beginning with Science

I will change directions slightly in the chapters that follow and introduce as much empirical and scientific content as possible, without getting mired in it, to advance my discussion of freedom. Empirical observation and the sciences are used in philosophy to maintain relevance and grounding. We have only our experiences to go on, which means philosophy should be grounded on them and scientific experiment from other fields, since in essence it needs to close the loop in the development of theories and come back to helping us shape our lives to be the most rewarding. We are intelligent in that we can learn from our experiences, extrapolate patterns and consistencies, and then use those to shape our futures. Any consequential theory needs to have relevance to human life, and for philosophy to ensure this it needs to ground itself on an empirical body of knowledge, the sciences. Although philosophical theories themselves cannot be tested empirically since they are abstractions of nature and experience, philosophy still needs to use the sciences and empirical phenomenon as the building blocks from which to form these structural abstractions. Because philosophy cannot be tested empirically, it must draw upon the sciences for support and inspiration to maintain a link to practical applicability. Just as the mind is the abstracted function of the neurological system, philosophy must be the abstracted interpretation of the sciences, as well as its guiding light.

To understand the degrees of freedom inherent in human behavior, I begin at its roots—current scientific understanding of the instincts. To understand the human instincts and their manifestations through impulses and drives, philosophy rests partly on sociological, psychological, and neuroscientific study. Sciences have the necessary means available for the possible future dissection of human behavior into that which is innate versus that which is developed; into that which is reducible to neurological explanation versus that which grows from experience; into that which stems from structures of systems versus that which stems from chance. Science has the mechanism by which to potentially unearth, through experimentation, the traits and needs that are universally innate to mankind, while philosophy has the freedom to structure these findings into a useful epistemology.

Psychology, sociology, neuroscience, and philosophy are mutually dependent fields, and the chapters that follow will draw from all these fields to come up with a holistic analysis of the basis of freedom. For example, many of the theories of Sigmund Freud, the famous father of early psychoanalysis, were actually taken from the philosophers of his time, including Schopenhauer and Nietzsche. Philosophy can and should drive psychological study, while philosophy needs some scientific grounding to be practical. Philosophy can then use scientific studies of human behavior to develop an epistemology to improve man's lot.

The Instinct Controversy

"It is held that the instincts lay down the basic and
permanent ends of human activity, and that human

intelligence is employed predominantly in so ordering behavior as to achieve the satisfactory attainment of these ends . . . All these writers [of theories on instincts] are agreed . . . that the major ends of human activity are rooted in the instincts." — Ronald Fletcher

The innate instincts are the genetically programmed seeds of human behavior that are universally held based on evolutionary selection. We are all born, in varying degrees, with a set of rules that ensure our survival and reproduction, along with the drives and physiology to enact them. All physiological organs and processes were created as fall-outs of evolutionary developments, just as the nervous system and its mental processes, including the instincts, were created as fall-outs of the same developments. All actions have intentions, and below our conscious understanding lies this instinctual intention to which we are not immediately privy, but which gives the underlying impetus behind our actions. The first step toward understanding the interaction between man and his environment is to understand his intentional disposition toward that environment, and thus to understand the innate instincts, the universal driving forces behind human behavior and development

The exact nature of man's instincts, however, is a controversial subject. Although I write as if they were a foregone conclusion, knowledge of the nature of their development and existence is anything but certain. Being mired in a society that is global in reach and influence, determining whether universal traits are universal because they are inherent (i.e., instinctual), or because they are taught equally across cultures according to long-entrenched roots, is difficult. Similarities in behavior could be due to human nature, or they could be due to cultural adaptation that gets transmitted across boundaries. The dissection of the human instincts is virtually impossible through current scientific means. An abstract understanding will have to suffice until new means are made available to the scientific community, as

Robert Wright states in his popular book on evolutionary psychology, *The Moral Animal*,:

> " . . . the general difficulty of explaining such universality [of a human trait] in utterly cultural terms is an example of how the Darwinian view, though not *proved* right in the sense that mathematical theorems are proved right, can still be the view that, by the rules of science, wins; its chain of explanation is shorter than the alternative chain and has fewer dubious links; it is a simpler and more potent theory."

This exact inability to rigorously and scientifically prove that certain behavioral traits are in fact human instincts made theories on instincts lose favor among the psychological community. Instincts manifest in us through means dependent on the culture and environment within which we were raised. Thus embedded and interpreted by our environments, instincts are difficult to isolate. Since we all live through a different set of experiences, a different combination of culture and environment, the different ways that the instincts can manifest becomes infinite, and thus difficult to isolate.

Suppose human females possessed a mothering instinct, for example. Depending on the nurturing nature of an individual female's mother, this instinct could either be fully repressed in the case of an abusive mother, or exaggerated in the case of a doting one. How could we determine, among an infinite range of other factors, whether the instinct was extant but environmentally manipulated, versus being merely taught by the mother? A person's mother is only one factor. How do you isolate the father, the siblings, the culture, etc.? And even if a substantial inherent female propensity towards mothering were shown, how would we define that propensity, and at what level of abstraction? Because of these questions, the psychological community became frustrated with the problem and abandoned it at large until some headway could be made.

Another example, the manifestation of the instinct to protect the self in the face of danger, will vary according to the dangers that are normally present in an individual's environment. An African Bushman will learn how to protect himself against predators while traversing dangerous terrain, while a city-person will learn as a pedestrian how to maneuver across streets during heavy traffic. Both are essential to survival, and both are learned through the impetus of the instinct to preserve the self's life. But it is difficult to uncover much more beyond this abstract description.

Behaviors are completely dependent upon the environment for context, but they are also dependent upon the instincts to provide the impetus for their development. I am not assuming that the will to live *necessarily* engendered these learned skills, but I am implying that these skills were not learned within a mental-intent vacuum. Nothing can be done or learned without a need or desire to provide the impetus. We, like computers, for example, need intent for everything—learning, moving, thinking, etc. A computer does nothing without human input. Lacking need and desire, it depends on humans to provide those in order to act and learn. Similarly, without instinctual impetus, we would not be able to determine what behaviors were important to learn versus which ones were inconsequential, and we would quickly wind up dead out of sheer maladaptive confusion and dysfunction. In other words, our instincts tell us that learning how to survive is good, and so we do so. When it comes to learning or acquiring a self-preserving impetus, trial and error would be a severely inappropriate heuristic. An error would be fatal by definition. Being born with this impetus is an intrinsic law of life.

The original instincts of a newborn get interpreted to fit the environment within which he is raised, and the situations within which he finds himself. Different cultures, different eras, different circumstances cause our development to interpret and manifest the instincts differently so that they are most apposite to ourselves and our environments. Instincts are highly adaptable to be useful, and thus difficult to track and isolate. The instinct becomes muddled through multiple and environment-dependent interpretations. Although its original intention remains intact, its manifestation is infinitely variable. Through observation we can formulate theories on the instincts' intentions, but proving our theories through a scientific method is difficult, especially given that we are biased observers, having the instincts we are studying inside ourselves.

Without an inherent way of finding, proving, and structuring human instincts, psychologists turned to other theories of human behavior for answers, such as Watson's Behaviorist[9] theories, for example. However, instinctual and evolutionary theory is starting to make a comeback, as can be seen by the rise in the number and popularity of evolutionist books. For example, Wright's *Moral Animal*, a book on evolutionary psychology, and Dr. Antonio R. Damasio's *Descarte's Error*, a book on neuroscience, both introduce theses where instincts play a vital role.

Although the difficulty of isolating the instincts has not disappeared, the persuasiveness and simplicity of the major categorizations of the instincts cannot be ignored altogether. This, coupled with the constantly improving neurophysiological information, experimenting techniques, and computerized models, creates the hope that deciphering the instincts will become more viable.

That instincts exist in some form has come to be largely accepted by the scientific communities, but anything beyond that becomes contentious. Only through the development of viable theories will the envelope of experimentation be pushed, and knowledge advanced.

The Instinct Hierarchy

As was discussed earlier, the crux of the controversy regarding instincts is that they are difficult to isolate. Scores of theories and books have been written about how to define the human

instincts and how to categorize them into groups and hierarchies, theories mostly written in the late nineteenth century
through the earlier part of this century. According to Fletcher,
one of the most famous theorists of instinctual theory was Sigmund
Freud. Freud categorized instincts mainly into two main groups—
the Life and Death instincts—although in general Freud's theories on instincts changed over time due to his dissatisfaction with
the subject. Unfortunate to instinctual theorists past, present, and
future, his theories, which by nature were untestable, pervaded
Western twentieth century thought. It is unfortunate because his
theories became practice without substantiation, dangerously
leading people in directions that at the least go nowhere, and at
the worst cause harm.

Only now that neurology has shone more light on the subject are instincts starting to be better grounded, now beginning
to shed the subjective categorizations of Freud and McDougall.
Previously unanswerable questions about instincts, such as, "Are
motor reflexes considered instincts?," "Are there hierarchies of
instincts or are they all loosely bound?," and "Are instincts considered integral or dichotomous to intelligence?" are now grounding themselves in neurology so that they are no longer completely
up to conjecture. Although science is still far from producing
concrete explanations, there now exist substantial links to neurology that in the future will pave the way to further experimentation.

Since Darwin's *The Origin of Species,* a substantial amount
of work has been undertaken to understand the role that instincts play in human interaction and development. Many different theories and ways of characterizing man's instincts exist, which
is a result of the vagueness of the definition of instincts and the
variability in their manifestation. Instinct, as a word, has been
used to describe everything from greed and jealousy to the desire for engendering children. Everything under the sun that has
been found to be widely encompassing has been termed instinctual at some point. Sorting out the ensuing mess of frameworks

---

[9] Behaviorism will be explained in more detail in Chapter Six

and definitions is beyond the scope of this book. Instead, let us
return to the original roots of instincts as a foundation upon
which to build the theories found herein.

Given that the nature of this book is philosophical and not
sociological, I will limit my introspection into the instincts to a
more abstracted view of the two most basic and prominent ones
in sociological and psychological literature. Since the categorization of instincts is highly theoretical, I will take a high-level
view to introduce my philosophical framework since the categorization of instincts is only important as far as it serves the purpose of presenting the philosophical theories. The two main instinct categories in this book are derived from Darwinian concepts.

The development of the theory of instincts came about by
and large as a corollary to Darwinian theory[10]. In his *Origin of
Species*, Darwin devotes a chapter to discussing instincts and
how they support his theory of natural selection. The basic tenet
of evolution is that the genes that create traits that are most successful in propagating themselves will be the ones that prevail[11].
In other words, the traits found in organic beings are traceable
to certain genes, and those traits that help the organic being to
reproduce and spread those genes the most will be the most
common and longest lived. In terms of life on earth, those traits
are reducible to those that either help the organism survive or
reproduce, for that is how the genes in the organisms prevail.
Although no earthly mandate compels genes to prevail, in order
for them to be found inside human DNA, it is a prerequisite. It is

---

[10] Other relevant theories regarding instincts existed prior to Darwin, but
Darwin's *The Origin of Species* is widely considered as the watershed.

[11] For a detailed explanation of this I recommend Dawkin's *The Selfish
Gene*. Basically put, all animal traits and characteristics exist for the sake
of protecting and reproducing the genes contained within the subject's
body, and not necessarily for the protection and reproduction of the individual being itself. For example, an animal seeks to protect the species
only insofar as there is a high correlation between the genetic makeup of
one animal in the species with the next. The animal is only protecting its
own genes found in another animal.

a prerequisite because otherwise genes would have not have been passed on to us by our biological ancestors.

Although I may at times anthropomorphize evolution, it is done merely as a writing tool or technique, rather than as an outshoot of my beliefs. As far as I can tell[12], no tenable guiding hand in life exists, no ultimate, external purpose, no Hegelian communal thread. Evolution does not necessarily take place as part of a natural plan, and does not have a unifying theme or intention. Living beings have come to evolve and exist not because of a larger evolutionary imperative, but rather because of ontological consequence. Either they take on traits that allow them to live, or traits that lead to their death. Those that live pass down their traits, those that don't survive, don't pass them down, and therefore the genes vanish from the gene pool. But no law states that living is either noble or necessary, nor that it is an evolutionary imperative. Evolution is simply an emergent consequence of the survivor's ability to pass down his own encoded traits. Not living, and not passing down traits, is neither bad nor good; neither right nor wrong; it just is. And evolution is neither bad nor good; neither right nor wrong; it just is. When I say genes or evolution in general cause things and manipulate beings into doing things, I'm stating it figuratively and not literally. Beings behave partially according to a set of rules imbedded in their genes that came to be as a result of eons of evolution, but the connection is neither causal nor intelligent. The connection is rather an abstraction in the opposite direction (from genetic trait to evolution), where evolution is instead an emergent quality of ontological causality. I imply a reverse causal connection (from evolution to genetic trait) merely as a writing technique that allows me to be more succinct.

The result of evolution is that the organisms today exist or are alive only because the organisms before them had the traits necessary to live long enough to survive and reproduce. We exist because our parents, our grandparents, our primal ancestors way before them, and everything in between, had the characteristics

---

[12] Being agnostic I do not believe in a larger intention, but I refuse to rule it out without proof one way or the other.

necessary to ensure two things: 1) that they could survive in their environment, and 2) that the duration of their survival was long enough for them to i) reproduce and ii) raise their progeny until that progeny could become sexually viable and independent. If any one of the members in our family tree had been either unfit to survive or been sexually impotent or uniquely unattractive, then we would have never been born. However, given that we are offsprings of that long family tree that did survive and reproduce, we too possess the traits necessary to ensure our survival long enough for reproduction and child raising, assuming no drastic event produced a punctured equilibrium[13]. We have their genes, and therefore similar characteristics and predispositions.

Those traits that prevailed and eventually evolved into man predetermine him to be rewarded for those behaviors or actions that increase the probability of survival, successful reproduction, and successful upbringing, at its most basic. According to Wright, for males sex is physiologically pleasurable, and lustful impulses ensure that an individual male seeks to maximize the amount of copulation he engages in his lifetime, therefore increasing the likelihood of passing on and multiplying his genes. Males are rewarded for copulation through pleasurable sensations. Similarly, they are rewarded for increasing their personal resource pool through positive sensations of pride and satisfaction. Personal wealth, taken in the loose definition of having anything that is valued by a society, is of paramount importance in the successful upbringing of progeny. The more wealth, the better the chances of having healthy children to pass on the parents' genes[14]. The highest-order instincts—such as the survival instinct theorized in evolutionary theory—manifest through human urges such as hunger and desire.

Behaviors and traits can be deconstructed into innate and developed systems of punishment and rewards aimed at manipulating the human being to ensure the multiplication of his genes.

---

[13] A punctured equilibrium is a drastic change in the development of a species that can be traced to cataclysmic environmental event, such as an asteroid pummeling the earth.
[14] Wright, pg. 67

Our urges and our physiological makeup—the systems of punishment and rewards—are evolution's way of ensuring that we adhere to the highest-order instincts, and are thus their animal manifestations. To reproduce and multiply we need to live and survive. To survive we must eat and breathe. And to eat and breath we need gastrointestinal and respiratory systems. In order to multiply, we must reproduce, and thus copulate. To induce us to copulate, we have developed or evolved sexual organs and impulses that make copulation pleasurable, thus rewarding us for engaging in it. Of course, this is only one among many ways that evolution induces us to copulate, but it is an apt example.

We are all different, however, in the degrees of punishment and rewards our bodies are programmed to dole out given the stimuli we encounter. Some of us might be adrenaline junkies, being greatly rewarded for facing and overcoming danger, while others of us might be paralyzed by phobias. In modern society phobias might be construed as excessive compensatory internal systems of punishment. However, the qualification that they are excessive can only be made in relation to the social norm. A careful balance exists between human traits and how society reacts to them. Although they may be considered excessive today, acute and neurotic fears may have been useful during prehistoric times of constant and insurmountable danger. Human traits, such as both the flight and fight responses, are seeded by the innate instincts, but their development is highly contingent on the environment.

How our traits develop, and how we interpret our environment, is strongly tied to the environment in which we are raised. For example, traits emphasizing physical endurance and lung capacity are physically rewarded, and thus more developed, in Tibetans living in the Himalayas. On the other hand, intellectual skills such as language-development abilities and logically structured thought would be emphasized in Silicon Valley. A programmer would be hard pressed to survive in the Tibetan Himalayas not just because he lacked the relevant knowledge of survival, but also because he probably lacked the physical characteristics to match.

The sustainment of life necessitates certain behavioral predisposition, and it is that predisposition that engenders the instincts. As Rousseau puts it, "Man's first law is to watch over his own preservation; his first care he owes to himself.[15]" Our future children depend upon our ability to survive long enough to reproduce and subsequently raise them, just as we depended upon our parents. The self-preservation instinct itself, though, is very broadly based, incorporating many different traits and characteristics that are all aimed at the ultimate survival of the individual. Evolution and natural social development build in animals and men a series of drives, needs, impulses, natural physical tools and weapons, and physiological processes, aimed at ensuring their survival. This includes drives such as hunger, impulses such as fight or flight, physical weapons such as horns, and general states of being such as desire.

The second predispositional instinct is to reproduce. If our ancestors had not copulated and reproduced, we would never have been born. All organisms exist because reproduction in one way or another is possible, and we exist because evolution has instilled an instinct into the human species that compels it to reproduce. Without reproduction, living organisms would have died out shortly after their conception in the primal soup. It, along with self-preservation, is an inherently necessary condition to sustain life on earth. All existing beings must have some innate characteristics that help them survive and reproduce, although in this book we will primarily concentrate on man's neurological characteristics and their consequent behavioral predisposition.

As Mihaly Csikszentmihalyi, the University of Chicago psychologist and author of books on "flow" (more on this later), states, evolution is the antithesis of entropy, trying to increase the complexity and integration of living systems on earth, rather than to increase chaos and dissipate energy. As living systems evolve, they become more complex through the specialization of func-

---

[15] From Rousseau's *Social Contract*, Book I, Chapter 2

tions and through the layering and abstraction of the interactions within and outside the living system. Cells within a body, and people within a society, for example, take on more specialized functions within the larger system, but their interaction with other cells or other people become more involved as communication and coordination gains importance. But as complexity increases, the more information needs to be stored or remembered regarding how to function within the system. The instincts, as well as the conscious mind, are the basic receptacles of information describing the function and interaction of the human animal with itself and its environment.

According to Csikszentmihalyi, the self, made up of both the instincts and the conscious mind, carries out two primary duties as an immediate function of evolution. First, to stop entropy from destroying any part of it, including its physical, mental, and social identities, and second, to reproduce itself physically, mentally, and socially.

Other traits, like the nurturing "instinct", may be deemed high-level instincts. The nurturing instinct is presumed to be the maternal and paternal instinct in humans to raise, protect, and emotionally attach themselves to not only their own children, but other human beings in general, and even animals and objects (like cars, for example). Like most of the other instincts, the nurturing instinct is controversial since it could be considered to fall under the main instincts, and thus not necessarily deemed to exist on its own at all.[16] The stratification and categorization of the impulses and instincts in man thus becomes a nearly impossible task, and so will not be considered here. Although instincts that fall entirely outside the umbrella of the two main ones mentioned may exist, they are not important to the thesis developed.

The two previously mentioned main instincts are the highest-order instincts from which all drives and impulses will be henceforth considered to flow. The fight-or-flight impulse, for example, can be considered to be derived from the instinct of preservation of one's own life. We have sexual and romantic im-

---

[16] Fletcher pg. 275

pulses and needs, but those are simple derivations of the instinct to reproduce. Regardless, most, if not all, impulses can be tied back to the manifestation of the two higher-order instincts, which are crucial to the creation, raising, and sustainment of human life.

Big Brother is Watching

Evolutionary theory has enjoyed popular support for some time in its description of the physical development of earthly species. Although it has had some challenges from religious orthodoxy ever since its conception, it has largely been held as accurate by the scientific community and the popular majority. However, when extending the theory to the psychological description of human behavior, only recently has evolution gained in popularity. On top of the traditional applications, evolutionary theory is now being used to describe the behavioral development of earthly species, particularly humans. The central theme is that natural selection not only filters on physical attributes, but on behavioral ones as well. Those innate behavioral traits that are broadly aimed at the successful growth and reproduction of the individual, and to some degree the species, have a natural advantage, just as certain physical traits give an individual a distinct advantage. When it comes to behavior, naturally selected instinctual dispositions are gaining ground in popular psychology and science as predictors and seeds of human behavior.

Scientific advancement has provided part of the drive behind the popularity of evolutionary psychology. Similarities between the innate processes of the animal brain and the human subcortical region[17] have been evinced through parallel work

---

[17] In order to not digress from the topic of this book, I will not go into neurophysiological detail. Suffice it to say, however, that the subcortical region of the brain, what Dr. Damasio uses to encapsulate the primal part of the brain, is mostly comprised of the limbic system. This system regulates the body and its processes, plays a part in the manufacturing of emotions and feelings, and is associated with the existence of instinctual drives.

between animals and humans. Both man and animal are born into the world with basic motor reflexes and homeostatic regulation. These processes are innate and instinctual, though they may also develop further with experience. For example, babies are born with the ability to regulate their own heartbeats and breathing, maintain chemical and hormonal balance, and even respond defensively to falling, or suck at the presence of a finger or nipple on their lips. These neurologically activated processes are innate, and thus demonstrate that at least at a basic level humans are born with some instinctual drives and response mechanisms.

Few people would argue with the above statement. However, the more controversial point made by Dr. Damasio applies to the existence of instincts that operate in the macro-regulation of both human behavior and the development of the brain and mind. His theory is logically persuasive, although perhaps still in the inchoate stages of broad-based experimental support[18].

Macro-regulation by the instincts implies that human innate mental processes are not restricted merely to the regulation of the body and basic survival instincts of babies, but also play a much larger role in the physiological development of the brain, and thus the psychological development of the mind. To put the connection into perspective, we must understand that the mind is simply the abstract conceptualization of the macro workings of the body's neurological system, including the brain. Any physiological impact on that neurological system, both the brain and the body, has a direct impact on its intangible model, the mind. Understanding the mind comes from understanding the brain and the interaction between brain and body. Brain damage, for

---

The neocortical region, on the other hand, is associated with the higher-order mental activities of the human brain, including language and the sensory systems.

[18] Actually, according to Fletcher (pg. 162-167), the bi-directional connection between the subcortical and the cortical regions of the brain, along with the ensuing link to the instincts, was postulated as far back as 1951 by Rudolph Brun in his General Theory of Neurosis, International Universities Press, Inc.

example, impairs specific functions of the mind, while physical mutilation of the body changes the interaction between the body and the mind, and alters the individual's concept of the self. Thus, any influence on the brain at a macro, non-homeostatic level will explicitly affect its function, and thus affect the mind's function. By stating that the instincts play a role in the macro-regulation of neurological processes beyond homeostatic regulation and its indirect impact, Dr. Damasio is implying a controlling or monitoring influence.

To put it in his own words, below is Dr. Damasio's introduction to the relationship between human development and human instincts:

> "The human genome (the sum total of the genes in our chromosomes) does not specify the entire structure of the brain . . . The disproportion [of genes to neurons and synapses] is not subtle: we carry probably about 10^5 (100,000) genes, but we have more than 10^{15} (10 trillion) synapses in our brains. Moreover, the genetically induced formation of tissues is assisted by interactions among cells . . . What happens among cells, as development unfolds, actually controls, in part, the expression of the genes that regulate development in the first place . . .
>
> The genome helps set the precise or nearly precise structure of a number of important systems and circuits in the evolutionarily old sectors [the subcortical region] of the brain . . . The principle role of the structure in these sectors is to regulate basic life processes . . . without which there is no survival . . . Yet there is another role for these innate circuits which I must emphasize because it usually is ignored in the conceptualization of the neural structures supporting mind and behavior: *Innate circuits intervene not just in bodily regulation*

*but also in the development and adult activity of the
evolutionarily modern structures of the brain."*

The genetic code that describes the creation and organization of the human body and brain is not long enough to precisely portray the arrangement of all the neurons and synapses.
Instead, the genetic code describes a standard blank-sheet arrangement for the neocortical or high-level regions of the brain,
and then, but more importantly, concentrates on the organization and structure of the critical subcortical region. Since the
subcortical region is critical to the minute-by-minute survival of
the individual, its advanced formation at birth is of high priority.
Remember that it is the subcortical regions of the brain that
keep the body in balance, the heart beating, the lungs breathing,
and as will be explored in more detail, keep the brain and body
focused on surviving the environment.

The detailed arrangements of the neocortical regions of the
brain, on the other hand, are formed by the experiences of the
individual through the assistance and rules set by the subcortical
region; they are not described by the individual's genetic makeup.
In essence, the neocortical regions at birth are akin to a one
pound mass of clay, and the subcortical regions are the tools by
which the sculptor—experience—develops the clay into shape.

" . . . genes also specify that the innate circuits [in
the subcortices] must exert a powerful influence on virtually the entire set of circuits that can be modified by
experience. That influence is carried out in good part
by "modulator" neurons acting on the remainder of the
circuitry . . . This clever arrangement can be described
as follows: (1) the innate regulatory circuits are involved
in the business of organism survival and because of that
they are privy to what is happening in the more modern
sectors of the brain; (2) the goodness and badness of
situations is regularly signaled to them; and (3) they

> express their inherent reaction to goodness and badness
> by influencing how the rest of the brain is shaped, so
> that it can assist survival in the most efficacious way."

According to Dr. Damasio the subcortices influence the physiological development of the brain in three ways: (1) by modulating the individual's perception of an experience; (2) by recording those experiences and responding to them according to a subcortical value system; and (3) by the formation of the value system itself. The subcortices determine whether something is beneficial or detrimental to the individual according to the value system. Events are then recorded and responded to according to the high-level rules determined by the system. This subcortical system developed because without a high-level set of criteria, the individual's naivete would ensure his death. It is in the individual's best interest to be born with a set of criteria by which he unconsciously lives in order to ensure his survival, his reproduction, and thus the propagation of his genes.

Although society teaches the individual the rules by which to live within it, the basic survival and reproduction instincts must be innate for the individual to endure independent of society. It is not necessarily in society's best interest to guarantee the survival of all its members, thus the individual must have a "magic hand," to borrow Adam Smith's term, guiding him. Very few people care if a specific member of a society lives or not, making it important for that individual to look out for himself. Evolution was too intelligent to leave the teaching of the tenets of survival and reproduction to family and society. Instead, in light of the possibility of being raised by negligent parents or hostile environments, evolution built in the survival and reproduction tenets. In hindsight, this seems like an obvious course for evolution to take, being that environments are highly variable and unpredictable.

Chaos theory has demonstrated that even where there seems to be randomness in nature, a seed or kernel exists by which that randomness occurs. Taking a broad enough view of a chaotic occurrence, one starts to see an underlying structure. So, too, with human behavior. As chaotic and random as people's actions may seem, a seeding kernel always exists, and thus the instincts impose an underlying structure. Everything that we do in our lives is influenced by our instincts and their enforcing directives.

Dr. Daniel Goleman, in his best-selling book *Emotional Intelligence*, describes in further detail the process by which the subcortical limbic system influences and monitors itself and the rest of the brain. The subcortices exert their influence by monitoring sensory information, influencing the individual's reactions, and prioritizing or strengthening a specific experience, memory, or response pattern. Goleman gives some insight into the process by which an experience gains priority in the brain using the research of Joseph LeDoux, a neuroscientist at the Center for Neural Science at New York University, as support. According to LeDoux's research, the amygdala, a key player in the brain's limbic system, acts as a tripwire and monitor of the sensorial activities of the brain. As Goleman explains:

> "In one of the most telling discoveries about emotions of the last decade, LeDoux's . . . research has shown that sensory signals from the eye or ear travel first in the brain to the thalamus, and then-across a single synapse-to the amygdala; a second signal from the thalamus is routed to the neocortex-the thinking brain. This branching allows the amygdala to begin to respond *before* the neocortex, which mulls information through several levels of brain circuits before it fully perceives and finally initiates its more finely tailored response."

The amygdala thus has a head start on the neocortex in responding to external stimuli. This head start gives the amygdala the ability to influence the neocortex's response, and allows it to influence the way in which the information is stored or memorized. The amygdala does this through its powerful influence over the brain and body in general, and the homeostatic regulatory regions of the brain specifically.[19] Through the complex interactions of the limbic system and the brain and body, the amygdala sets the stage by which the brain and body's response is carried out. The amygdala can heighten specific brain functions and senses, alter the mood and energy levels of the individual as a whole, induce into action various vascular, respiratory, and skeletal muscles, and change the composure of the individual's visage, including facial expression and skin dampness and sensitivity. All these combined factors then powerfully influence the ultimate response and behavior of the individual.

For example, it would be difficult to respond calmly to a threatening situation if our faces were flush and grimacing, if we had an explosive amount of energy coursing through our veins, if our respiration and heartbeats were actuating at furious paces, if all the muscles in our torsos, arms, and fists tensed up, and if our vision and hearing grew painfully acute. Even the falling of a pin would set us off in this physical composure—the exact composure in which our limbic system has placed us. Although exaggerated, the above mentioned subcortical response is exactly one of the ways in which the neocortex is influenced into a preferred reaction. An aggressive response would become more probable, while our more inert responses would become less so.

The amygdala also influences behavior through the way in

_____

[19] According to Goleman "From the amygdala, projections extend out to every major part of the brain. From the central and medial areas a branch goes to the areas of the hypothalamus… which mobilizes the fight-or-flight reaction via a cascade of… hormones. The amygdala's basal area sends out branches to the corpus striatum, linking into the brain's system for movement. And, via the nearby central nucleus, the amygdala sends signals to the autonomic nervous system via the medulla, activating a wide range of far-flung responses in the cardiovascular system, muscles, and the gut. The amygdala [also influences the]… cells that regulate the large muscles of the skeleton[,]… overall reactivity of the brain areas that receive [norepinephrine]… [etc.]"

which it regulates the storing and learning of experiences and information. First, by having a head start in the perception of sensory information, the amygdala has the ability to set the emotional stage under which the sensory information will be perceived[20]. The amygdala can influence how we perceive something by putting it under a positive or negative emotional light, and by the intensity of the emotional light. We would tend to be biased toward an experience that we associate with intense feelings of elation, versus one that we associate with sadness or anger, or even versus one that merely makes us glad. We would rather do or think of something that made us happy, versus doing or thinking of something that made us sad. The happiness-inducing reactions become accentuated in the mind, and the sadness-inducing ones get attenuated.

In addition to the different types of emotions, the amygdala also influences behavior through the modulation of the strength or intensity of a memory. As Dr. Goleman explains:

> "The brain uses a simple but cunning method to make emotional memories register with special potency: the very same neurochemical alerting systems that prime the body to react . . . also stamp the moment in memory with vividness. Under stress (or anxiety, or presumably even the intense excitement of joy) a nerve running from the brain to the adrenal glands atop the kidneys triggers a secretion of the hormones epinephrine and norepinephrine, which surge through the body priming it for an emergency. These hormones activate receptors on the vagus nerve; while the vagus nerve carries mes-

---

[20] Note that Dr. Damasio differentiates between the type of preemptive emotion described here, which he dubs "primary" emotion, and that which is induced by recall, which he dubs "secondary" emotion. Primary emotions, according to Dr. Damasio, are the visceral emotions, which are a reflex to stimuli, emanating from the amygdala, and include emotions such as fear and anger. Secondary emotions are induced in the brain and body as part of thought or memory recall, and involve processing by the neocortex.

sages from the brain to regulate the heart, it also carries
signals in to the brain, triggered by epinephrine and
norepinephrine. The amygdala is the main site in the
brain where these signals go; they activate neurons within
the amygdala to signal other brain regions to strengthen
memory for what is happening.

This amygdala arousal seems to imprint in memory
most moments of emotional arousal with an added degree of strength. . . ."

Thus, the subcortical regions influence future behavior by
associating experiences and learned responses with an emotion,
and then they further impart influence over learned behavior
and experiences by designating the strength or vividness of the
memory. How does the subcortical brain know how intense and
under what type of emotion to record an event? The subcortical
brain must contain a set of criteria by which it determines what
is appropriate and what is not, what is important and what is
not. As you know by now, that set of deterministic rules are the
instincts, a set of criteria by which we unknowingly experience
life, remember it, and react to it. It is ultimately up to the subcortical regions of the brain, and the built-in instinctual laws of life,
to determine the appropriate emotional and memorization response to stimuli.

Instincts, Learning, and Intelligence

Beginning strongly at birth and continuing with less intensity
throughout the rest of life, our brains are metaphorical sponges
soaking in information, processing it, storing it, and replaying it.
We live to experience things so we can learn from those experiences and in turn adapt ourselves more effectively to our environment. Every experience we have, every piece of information

we store, every response we activate is aimed at improving our effectiveness in fulfilling our main instincts.

Again, at birth, our cortical regions are a metaphorical blank slate. This slate is designed to be filled by the individual's experiences through the careful monitoring and guidance of the subcortical regions. We learn from our experiences and behave according to how those experience have shaped us, all under the supervision of our instincts. Our inquisitive natures reflect our need, and desire, to learn. Beyond the internal influences, these shaping experiences are also widely influenced by the society within which we are immersed, helping us adapt to such society

Although born relatively ignorant, we still come into the world with the essential neurological processes needed to regulate homeostasis and develop and mature both physically and mentally. It is impossible to be taught how to learn: to be taught how to conduct electrical signals and arrange synapses to record, process, and regurgitate information, or to be taught how to focus the senses and internally impart importance on certain information over another. The learning process needs to be, and is, inherent in the physiological makeup and innate programming of the nervous system.

How we learn, what we learn, how we associate and link thoughts, and how intensely we learn, is all governed by our internal programmed objectives, our instincts. However, what is determined to be detrimental versus what is beneficial to the individual vis-à-vis the instincts is of course adapted from the environment and surrounding culture. For example, we aren't born knowing that smoking is hazardous to our health, our culture teaches us that. In fact it used to be thought to be benign, and even beneficial because of its relaxation effect. Smoking was far more prevalent then. Of course we all place different importance on different factors, and for some the pleasurable act of smoking and the attractiveness of the act is more important than the associated health risks, while for others the health risks outweigh other considerations. Whether we determine smoking to be beneficial or detrimental is ruled by environmental factors, but our reaction to that determination is made according to internal guidelines.

An important sidebar fact to remember in the smoking example is that survival of the individual, and indirectly-speaking, his general health, are not the end-all of his existence. The instincts' intents seem deceptively simple based on how they've been laid out here, but remember that the manifestation of the instincts is immeasurably complex since they are inextricably tied to the environment. If the instincts' only intent were survival, then no one would ever think of smoking. The broader justification behind the creation of the human form, and any living organism for that matter, is the perfection of a gene-protecting and duplicating machine. We exist because we are of great use to our genes. Thus, the duplication of our genes through reproduction is also important, if not more so. If smoking can help us look attractive to the opposite sex according to the society that deems it so, then naturally we would expect a considerable portion of the population to smoke.

According to genetics and environment we place varying levels of importance to the different factors that determine how we learn, and in turn how we behave. Past societies considered smoking attractive, being associated with the Marlboro Man and James Dean, "cool" and rebellious images. As we were then, and as we are now, we are dependent on the environment to supply the substance behind experience. As the environment or society changes, the average individual's behavior changes accordingly. Attitudes towards smoking today are different from those in the 1950's.

We are thus dependent upon society to teach us to adapt our instincts to survive. We are dependent upon it to interpret our environment, and to teach us how to interact with those around us so that we can do that which we were born to do: to survive, to find and attract those of the opposite sex so we can reproduce, and then provide the means to raise the children we beget[21].

We are dependent on society to provide people of the opposite sex with whom to reproduce, and thus we must play by its rules if we are to get what we seek. We depend on it to acquire any type of wealth, and again, must thus learn how to play and succeed by its terms. We are inextricably tied to society, and consequently so is our internal system of rewards and punishments. Our higher-order instincts manifest themselves in ways we learn by experience, and thus in ways that are taught by society.

We are thus born dependent on family and on society. How the environment, a large part of which is the people with whom we were raised, impacts us, will help determine what makes us happy, sad, and what will fulfill us.

As Fletcher puts it:

> "Whilst believing that the permanent basis of human life is instinctive, Hobhouse[22] conceives the instincts in man as being of the nature of innate promptings, cravings, or determining tendencies, which are specific in themselves but which do not comprise fixed inherited motor-patterns of behavior. The actual overt pattern of behavior which is manifested in efforts to satisfy these promptings is not automatically given, to the same degree as in the lower species, but depends largely upon the experience and intelligent control of the individual and also *upon the complex influences of the social tradition into which he is born and within which he lives.*"

We are born with "promptings, cravings, and determining

---

[21] I am not implying any connection between the natural rationalization of life and morality. Being great gene-reproduction machines does not mean we need, nor have to fulfill that role. Celibacy and homosexuality hold neither more nor less meaning than Mormonism to an unintelligent gene and its enforcer, the instinct.

[22] L.T. Hobhouse, *Social Development,* London, 1924

tendencies," but the actual exhibited behavior is learned through experience, adapted from those around us. Since we are constantly interacting with people, and society in general, our experiences are completely tainted by cultural influence. Thus, in order to understand and harness our instincts, we must understand the interrelationships between the individual and his society. In this understanding, the act and process of learning is of paramount importance.

The learning process is the nervous system's method of absorbing and adapting to experience. The instincts play a heavy hand in that process, and thus in the overall acclimatization and response to experience. Thus, the instincts play a multifaceted role in the individual's ability to interact with his environment. They supply the original impetus to act, they set the tone under which the experience is viewed, and they regulate the process under which behavior is adapted and learned.

A Need for Society

Social dependence begins from the moment we are born. We depend on others to completely take care of us as babies, and then we depend on them to teach us how to survive as we grow up. As humans, we are among the most defenseless animals at birth, born without even the slightest ambulatory capacities. Born without any particular physical advantage outside of our brains, we depend wholly on the development of our minds for survival. Whereas animals have speed, size, strength, and weapons such as antlers, or protective gear such as shells, we are wholly vulnerable without our ingenuity.

Human development, although guided by the higher-order instincts, is also highly dependent on experience. Where animals exhibit complex instinctual behavioral patterns, such as nest infestation in the case of the cuckoo bird and migration behavior in the case of the salmon, we exhibit very little beyond homeostasis. As babies and children we depend on our families and societies to teach us how to survive and master our environment. Although we may be born with the ability to hunger for food, we depend on others to teach us how to find it, catch it, hunt it, prepare it, and cook it. Without these teachings, and without the initial support of our families, we would die of hunger. Although we are born with the instinct to survive and reproduce, we must be taught how to manifest those instincts depending on our environments. Having the instincts means nothing if we do not know how to apply them later on.

As adults, we depend on others to help us secure the resources necessary for survival. We have the physical characteristics and prowess to survive on our own, but they are not enough when raising a family. We cannot hunt, farm, provide security for our family, and raise children all by ourselves. We depend on a society to help us share those tasks. Even the most independent pioneers, settlers, and frontiersmen of early U.S. history maintained loose ties to each other for mutual support and out of need. Early Homo Sapiens required the formation of communities for protection and security. As a family, and thus as a race, we need and depend on communities for survival and growth. As a response to this mutual need of other people, evolution has developed internal programming to ensure our roles in society, to ensure that we help society flourish, and therefore to ensure our own survival.

Because man relies on society for his survival, culture, at the impetus of the instincts, inculcates into him the traits necessary to ensure the survival of society. For the race to survive—and herein lies the impetus of the survival instinct in respect to our genes—man needs to form and protect some form of common society. One of those traits formed by a mix of culture and instinct is the need for self-worth or valuation. As will be explored further in later sections, the need to feel valuable would ensure that we as individuals do things of value to the society, such as become entrepreneurial and perform acts of charity. Our need for self-worth would ensure that we benefit society by improving others' lots through whatever skills and means available to us, be it innovation, charity, governance, or other means. We need to feel as though we are of value to those around us. To some extent, culture and evolution have developed this internal need to ensure the success of society, and since man is dependent on society, for our own success.

As was alluded in previous chapters, and will be discussed in more detail in future ones, an intrinsic characteristic of the instincts is to measure the relevance of phenomena against its own intentions through systems of weighting or valuation. In other words, the instincts influence us into a course of action at a level of intensity that differs according to some internal system of relative weights and measures. All phenomena, including social phenomena, must go through these valuations in order for the instincts to impute the right response.

The interaction between our ineluctable need for others and our intrinsic instinctual imperatives results in the formation of a need to feel valuable to society. Since we depend on society to survive and reproduce, and those are our internal imperatives — to survive and reproduce — then it follows that we have adapted our behavior to maximize the utility of our relationship with society. In other words, we have created internal behavioral systems to ensure that we can get the most out of our relationship with society. I say "we" have created these things because I'm assuming that the relationship is extrinsically driven. I am loosely assuming that no explicit instinctual regulation of our social interactions exist above and beyond the regulation of the two high-level instincts, but rather that these internal regulatory systems are environmental adaptations of the two instincts to our constant immersion in society. Whether the resulting behavioral systems are extrinsically driven, or inherently internalized through evolution, is difficult to say. What is not difficult to say is that these systems of value exist in man in one form or another.

Regardless of the source of the social behavioral systems,

our immersion in society, along with the instincts' internal system of value, create a reciprocal internal system of valuation. This reciprocal system measures the success of our relationship with society and vice versa. Since we each have different strengths, skills, needs, and upbringings, we each have reciprocal valuation systems that apply different type and weights of values to ourselves. What value we place on ourselves and our actions is completely subjective and varies from person to person. What is mortally important to one individual could be irrelevant to the next.

Once we determine our own level of comfort with the freedoms we allow ourselves, it is important to apply those freedoms toward deriving the most value out of our relationships with society. We have determined that we have an internal behavioral system from which we derive value vis-à-vis society. The next step is to understand that subjective system. Once we understand how we derive value, we can either adapt our behavior to derive the most value, or we can try to manipulate that system.

Validation and Adaptation

In later chapters we will see that as humans we are fallible in every way. And, even as flexible and adaptive as the instincts are, they too can at times misjudge. The instincts are not necessarily God's will, and their application in life is neither right nor wrong. That the "instinct is not always perfect in its working; that it does not proceed on an unchangeable model; that it is on occasion applied mistakenly, uselessly and injuriously; that it is often incomplete at birth, and requires development . . ."[23] is a testament to its fallibility. Instincts, like social laws, provide direction and rules of execution, but when applied throughout a lifetime of experience, will at times be inappropriate or conflicting.

Again, take smoking. Although it is injurious, addictive, and antithetical to the survival instinct, its pleasurable effects and

---

[23] L.T. Hobhouse, *Social Development*, London, 1924

social attraction, and thus its enticement through the manifestation of vanity by the instincts, are too strong for a reasonably significant portion of the population. We are not programmed, and with good reason, to give too much weight to long-term consequences, in this case the future probability of addiction and injury. The good reason is that the further out in the future something lies, the smaller its probability of occurrence, thus naturally the less weight we apply to it. However, we have an inexplicable bias of giving too much weight to immediate gratification. This may be due to the fact that the bias developed during the caveman days, when the future was highly unpredictable and planning and forecasting was done primitively. As with the case of smoking, depending upon our views on longevity versus hedonism, we might say our judgement fails us. The need for immediate gratification is stronger than the possibility of harm some ways down the road.

In the cases of smoking or consuming harmful drugs, a skewed conflict exists between instincts. But as was alluded, a second factor also causes the misapplication of the instincts. The instincts and human physiology may also misfire since biological evolution is far slower than human advancement. We smoke, overeat, and in general overindulge because we evolved in environments where we went through constant cycles of scarcity followed by overabundance. We were designed to overindulge during periods of overabundance to prepare for the periods of scarcity. The problem now, however, is that we Westerners now live in societies where resources are in constant plentitude. We overindulge because we can and are naturally inclined to do so. This overindulgence leads to obesity, which has been determined to be a causal factor in many, serious health problems.

Our instincts, our senses, and our minds are fallible in their abilities to relate effectively with our environment, including society, thus all need constant calibration and confirmation. To compensate for this fallibility, we have developed intricate feedback mechanisms to constantly keep us on track. Our perceptions and our behavior are constantly being validated by ourselves against external sources..

Learning and soaking in information from experience is in and of itself useless if the information is not filtered, processed, and validated. Our instincts play the role of filters and processors of information. Being internal and completely subjective, however, they cannot also execute the role of validating information, especially since they themselves are subject to error. Validation by definition requires an external, non-biased source. We therefore cannot rely on ourselves to validate what we learned, how we processed it, and the effectiveness of the manifestation of what we have learned and processed. What we need is exactly the source from which we have learned, our environment in general, and society specifically. Society, friends, family, and the people in the world at large are best equipped to inform us if what we do and say is the most effective way of getting what we need and want.

Being trapped behind a subjective sensorial world where the veracity and accuracy of everything perceived comes into question, we seek the validation of what we perceive as reality from everyone and everything surrounding us. We cannot prove that the reality we perceive is in effect an absolute reality, but having people, as well as animals, recognize us, agree with us, like us, and react to us, makes us feel as though our identities as human beings and the realities we perceive have been validated. The more people we can get to attest to our existence, the more our existence is validated. The more our existence is validated, the more we feel "alive."

Philosophically, this translates to the self's dependence on others for its own revelation. It is only through interaction with others that the self can project itself, be validated, and thus be revealed. The concept of the self would lose meaning in a vacuum. In other words, without a "you" or a "them," there is no "me." This goes back to the concept that light cannot exist without darkness, that things need a contrast to gain definition. The self needs contrasting selves to gain identity. The more it interacts with others, the more it gains an identity. Although we do not necessarily need a *human* other to reveal our selves, we do need human others to reveal our human selves. Interacting with a dog would be enough to reveal our separate selves, but to the dog we are nothing but another animal. We would not have been able to reveal our humanity since the dog can neither identify our human characteristics, nor mirror them. Intelligence and spirituality are incomprehensible to a dog, and thus useless as far as communication goes. He can react to us independently, and thus reveal that as a self we exist, but that is the extent of the result of our interaction. To reveal our human selves, and thus simply to exist as humans, we need to interact with other beings able to identify our human characteristics, which for now limits us to interaction with other humans to validate our own humanity. The larger extent to which this is possible, with the more people and with greater emotion, the more intense the validation.

Validation even applies beyond our external characteristics to personal phenomena, such as the validation of our own feelings. The people around us have a large amount of sway in how we view ourselves and our thoughts and emotions. For example, we can come to doubt whether something makes us happy or sad if everyone around us tells us it does not. We come to believe we are confused about ourselves and behave in a way that is expected. As a further example, we might meet someone and offhand find him or her attractive. In time, though, with enough people telling us otherwise, we might change our feelings and wind up finding that person unattractive.

As David Hume explained in *An Inquiry Concerning Human Understanding*, reality implies believing those things that we deem most probable. This implies that as we try to posit a reality, we seek to validate the probability of something through the acknowledgement of phenomena by those people around us, as well as through supporting evidence. The more something is acknowledged, and the larger the amount of supporting evidence, the more comfortable we become in believing it. The caveat is that people might ignore some evidence, or give too much weight to another, to appease internal or external expectations. But in general we tend to calibrate and validate our internal thoughts and emotions, and our external behavior, by monitoring the responses of the people and environments around us. Positive responses reinforce thoughts, feelings, and behavior; negative responses attenuate them.

The more people we can get to attest to our effective adaptation into society, the more that adaptation is validated. Thus we crave fame, love, and adoration since they are all forms of validation. We crave fame because of the numbers involved. The larger the number of people that recognize us, and thus validate us, the more we feel successful at having adapted our instincts to society. But we also crave love, which is partly derived from the weight assigned to the opinion of those we know. The more someone loves us, the more weight we assign to their opinion, the more we feel validated. In other words, when someone loves us, they are validating us with more weight than when does a stranger.

Social validation implies a dependency on society for happiness, social status, and every other facet of life touched by other people. Since we depend on extrinsic validation of our internal mental mechanisms and our external behavior to keep us attuned and on track with our environment, then it follows that we are necessarily dependent on our environment, notably society, to provide that function. This necessary dependence implies an obligation to maintain an ongoing relationship with our encompassing society. In order to receive validation, we need to have open relationships that allow the communication of that validation. If we could not communicate with our environment, and therefore were unable to interpret its signals, then we would not be able to judge whether our adaptation to our environment and the manifestation of our instincts were successful or not.

Thus, in order to properly function within society we need to adapt to its methods of communication, methods that become the frameworks under which we structure and define life.

As babies we learn verbal and body language to communicate effectively. But language is a dynamic and constantly changing entity that we never stop learning. Every job, every ethnicity, every region has a different jargon and different interpretation and use of language, and to thrive within each different pocket of society we are constantly having to learn the new jargons. We constantly need society not only to teach us how to communicate, but also to validate that what we have learned is correct or still applicable. Validation becomes a crucial component as we continuously check that we have learned and understood correctly, and then in turn are also applying it correctly.

Language becomes an integral part of validation. The definitions of objects and phenomena carry with them the structure through which thought and behavior becomes validated. Definitions in general carry the weight of history and culture, specifically the attitudes and dispositions toward objects and phenomena. Definitions can have positive or negative undertones, covering abstract or specific range. The extent to which we absorb these undertones and ranges determines our level of synchronization with the surrounding culture, and thus its validation to our level of adaptation. This ensuing validation through language greatly impacts our thoughts and behavior. Generally speaking, how something is defined dictates its impact on our lives. For example, happiness is defined differently according to different cultures, and therefore what makes a person happy changes according to the culture and the language. We depend on society to define happiness, and we depend on society to validate our happiness according to that definition. We say we are happy when we meet that and we allow ourselves the repercussions of such a statement once our definition is validated. In American society professional success is largely deemed to be a determinant of happiness, and thus an inherent part of its definition. People are industrious in their search for success and ultimate happiness. Making sacrifices for a job is rewarded and reinforced; to lack ambition is unattractive and attenuated in behavior.

We depend on society to teach a word to us, we live by its definition, and we depend on society to validate our interpretation of the definition. Thus our dependence on society is reinforced. We depend on it to teach us to communicate, to validate what we have learned, and to validate our experiences. In essence, we are products of the different forms of communication. To break the norms of language is to create barriers to communication, ensuring our failure within society.

Communication is not the only thing we adapt and validate from society. Our behavior itself is based on what we learn from our experiences and how we adapted our instincts according to them. We learn how to respond to situations depending on how we or others responded to similar situations in the past. We vary our response according to the differences between the new situation and those past situations, but regardless we are still reacting to the environment and mimicking learned response patterns. Thus we not only learn to define happiness linguistically, for example, we also learn to define it empirically and by the situations that evoke it, to then know to respond by feeling happy. We learn to recognize what situations make us happy, and which ones do not. And then we validate if our "happy" response to those certain situations is appropriate or not by witnessing people's reaction to our response.

When a child is growing up, for example, the surrounding people encourage him to play one certain sport over another. By playing this sport he receives smiles and encouragement; thus he tries harder. With this encouragement and subsequent effort, the child develops a facility and affinity for the sport. But beyond this positive reinforcement, the child also feeds off of the happy atmosphere and jovial responses to the sport by the parents. He learns to feel happy and respond jovially according to those responses The child has learned to feel happy when engaged in that sport, be it playing, watching, or even discussing it. The sport will now become part of the child's larger definition of happiness. Contrasted to that, the parents will probably not encourage the child to play other sports or do other activities as much as those they did as children. Having learned to be encouraged in certain ways and discouraged in others, the parents will mimic the behaviors of their parents and act respectively[24]. Of course, part of the parents' bias comes from the fact that they have more knowledge and vested interest in the things they themselves did as children. But sports is only one facet of parenting that parents learn from their childhoods and then mimic accordingly. To some extent this is also true about other things, such as methods of punishment, political views, and so on.

A more encompassing example involves the learned response of showing embarrassment. In American culture, people blush and take on a surprised or sheepish appearance when embarrassed. In eastern China, in contrast, people are accustomed to smiling when presented with an embarrassing situation. Where an American would blush, a Chinese would smile. More often than not American tourists in China become frustrated when confronted with a hotel clerk that begins to smile from ear to ear after hearing of a problem with the room or facilities. To the American, the Chinese appears to be flippant, standing there smiling and listening while the tourist vents. To the Chinese, the American appears to be rude, getting louder and more obnoxious as he complains. Neither response is right nor wrong; they are both ingrained in the society and learned from it.

We are neither inherently programmed to smile, nor to react sheepishly, in order to show embarrassment. Both responses are learned from observing those around us as we grow up. Similarly, we are not born to feel sad nor angry with pain, we are merely born to sense discomfort and the effects from the ensuing autonomic responses, such as the sympathetic and humoral re-

---

[24] A child may also do the opposite and rebel against a parents' influence. Either way, the child is developing in response to his environment, most notably his parents, whether the response is positive or negative.

sponses[25]. We learn to interpret both as feelings of sadness or anger, while masochists actually interpret pain as arousing and exciting. These are not programmed responses, but learned ones. The correction or enforcement of these learned responses occurs when they are either validated and encouraged or rejected. Misinterpretation by a person of his environment is not uncommon, thereby making validation an important correctional tool.

People seek validation of their actions as a way to confirm that their behavior is in tune with the society and the culture within which the person is immersed. Validation confirms or denies the person's ability to learn from, and adapt to, his surroundings. Without the validation the individual might act in discordance with the social norms because of misinterpretation of the norms or because of a maladaptive response. Without the correction in behavior the person will suffer rejection and ridicule. Validation is a way for the individual to catch problems and correct them.

It is important to learn the effects (learned response patterns, adaptation of the instincts, and the search for validation) that society foists upon us and their connection to our instincts in order to not be prisoners of both. We all need, and immutably must to some basic degree, absorb and reflect the tenets of communication and the behavioral norms of our encompassing society. The degree and extent to which this is true, however, is up to us. Forms of communication and behavioral norms can be liberating if used as tools, but also limiting in the structure they impose.

Our challenge is to use the tools and transcend the structure.

---

[25] The sympathetic and humoral responses are physiological mechanisms that mediate involuntary reactions to the environment through the regulation of many body processes

Cutting the Strings

The one thing for certain is that we are humans bound to the physiological processes that breathe life and death into us. Our hearts are the engines of our circulatory systems, which transfer nutrients to our bodies so we can live and thrive. Our lungs are the engines of our respiratory systems, which supply and remove gases from our bodies so we can live and thrive. Our instincts are the engines of our behavior, which allow us to interact with our environment so we can live and thrive. Just as we cannot remove our hearts or lungs and live, we cannot remove our instincts.

But our instincts are more essential than that. More than our circulatory or respiratory systems, our behavior encapsulates what or who we are. Like the genes within our cells that at each moment create us physically, the basic instincts imbedded in our brains at each moment create us metaphysically. Our bodies are created according to our genetic structures, and our behaviors are created according to our instinctual structures. To try to remove or change our instincts is to try to leave a tree intact but remove its roots. What remains is no longer a tree but a log. Without are instincts we would no longer be humans but automatons, bound to reacting without purpose, mimicking without evolving.

It is not that we are trapped or imprisoned by the structure inherent in our instincts, but rather that we are given life through it. If alternatives to our instincts existed, an alternative life to one of being human, then we could say we were being bound because our choices were being restricted. But there is no outside option. Our choice is life, and with it all that being human means, including having hearts, lungs, and instincts. Having this structure around our behavior is liberating in that it gives us life and all the options that come with it.

Living by the rules, however, is different from using the rules to live. We have this amazing power of self-awareness that gives us the ability to know [...] how things influence us so we can influence their [...] through which we are influenced. To know ourselves is to have some power over ourselves and who we are. We can use the instincts and their mechanisms to our own advantage to help shape our own behavior. Obviously, we have no way of influencing the internal physiological processes of regulation and modulation (maybe through drugs), but we are privy to the inputs and outputs: our experiences, valuation systems, and resulting responses. Previously we discussed how the instincts prepare and bias the body towards a response to an experience by setting the body in an emotional state, and by stamping the experience in memory with a given emotion and intensity. This is the process that biases the output, done according to a set of guidelines or values held by the instincts. This chapter will talk about our capabilities to influence the described process through the inputs, and next chapter will discuss the influencing of our intrinsic valuation system, i.e., the rules and guidelines of the process.

One of the inputs to the process of creating behavioral inclinations is the emotional setting and the intensity within which we come to experience an event. In general we know what tends to make us happy, satisfied, sad, tired, energized, etc. By concomitantly placing events that we know yield a certain emotional state with those that we want to equate with that same state, we influence our behaviors through our dispositions. We can thus influence our behavioral patterns by modulating our perceptions of experiences. After a while we come to have similar dispositions for those events we place concomitantly. For example, let us imagine we have an affinity for chocolate, plus a desire to exercise more. By eating small amounts of chocolate before or during exercise we are able to impose the pleasant states of emotion derived from chocolate onto exercise, influencing our future disposition towards exercise. That influence will be stronger if we only eat chocolate when we exercise since the positive marginal effects of eating chocolate are larger (in

other words, we enjoy every bite more if we eat chocolate spar-
ingly). Of course we might also have the opposite effect as well
of equating chocolate with whatever feelings we get when we
exercise, perhaps reducing our affinity for chocolate. But in essence, we are able to influence our future behaviors by altering
our dispositions toward events or phenomena.

We can also influence the intensity of our dispositions by the
intensity of the emotional states within which the different events
we choose place us. In other words, we might have a strong
affinity for chocolate, but only a slight liking of candy. We can
choose to eat candy versus chocolate when we exercise to only
get a slight affinity.

We do not actually have to do something physical, though,
to obtain a desired effect or emotion. As will be explored in
more detail later, we can activate emotions by simply thinking of
or remembering events or scenarios. We do not have to eat a
chocolate to get the pleasant feelings and emotions associated
with it. We can remember eating chocolate, and those memories will induce the emotions in us. Instead of eating chocolate,
we can think of eating it while we exercise. The problem, though,
is that the emotions induced through memory are only slightly as
intense as the live experience. Just thinking of chocolate might
not be enough to change my disposition even slightly, especially
if exercising is so demanding that it makes thinking difficult. It
would be more effective to simply eat a small bite.

Just as memories evoke milder emotions, so it is that memories themselves and their associated emotions are easier to influence. As will be discussed later, memories are malleable and
prone to suggestion. It is easier to influence a past memory than
to influence the creation of a new one. By merely focusing on
the bad or good aspects of objects or phenomena in memory,
we can impact our dispositions toward them. In the example of
exercising, we can also improve our dispositions by thinking of
their positive aspects, such as the feeling of pride or the achieve-
ment of milestones. This will improve our memorized disposi-

tions toward exercise so that we may in fact look forward to it. It takes mental work to actively remember good or bad aspect of things, but if important enough, we can influence our own behaviors.

Although similar, this is not necessarily Pavlovian association. Pavlov always fed his dog immediately following the ringing of a bell in his much-renowned experiment. In time, the dog came to equate the ringing of that bell with feeding time, salivating every time Pavlov rang it. The dog associated the one event with another, assuming through his experience that the cause, the ringing of the bell, always had the same effect—the delivery of food. This is tantamount to equating jumping up with falling down. As rational beings we assume, according to our experience, that the cause, jumping up, will always be followed by the effect, falling back down.

The Pavlovian linking of events is different from what I am discussing here, which is the changing of the emotional disposition stamped on a memory or behavior. The desired effect is not for the person in the example to associate exercise with chocolate (winding up with a craving every time he exercises), but rather for the person to play an active role in how the mind forms emotional dispositions toward behaviors by means of concatenating events. The concatenating of events are a method toward an end, not the end itself. The person in the example could rotate pleasant experiences every time he exercises, such as watching a favorite sport, getting kisses from a loved one, or whatever. The importance lies in the emotional stamp the behavior receives so that his future behavior is altered; so that he may feel better about exercising to make it easier to do it in the future.

The conditioning of internal dispositions toward phenomena can only occur when the intent is real, however. I am not implying in the above examples that a person can make himself want to exercise by event concatenation. Rather, I am saying that a person can come to *feel* differently about exercise to make it easier. If the person does not have a real desire to exercise or enjoy its benefits, no amount of emotional stamping can change his desire. The desire must be original to create an impetus. We cannot fool ourselves, we can only influence. If, on the other hand, the person does have a desire to exercise, but has a problem with motivation, positive emotional stamping will help.

From Drone to Man

A more basic way of gaining control over our own behavior is by changing our paradigmatic dispositions toward emotional states, responses, words, and anything else that plays a part in creating our behavior. Instead of influencing the emotional stamp placed in memory, we can also change the way we feel about or see the stamp itself. As was discussed in the previous section, we depend on society to teach us the rules and norms of behavior in order to live and thrive within it. Society teaches us how to interpret our environment and how to communicate with it. We are taught language so that we can communicate with each other to reap the fruits of sharing. But within each word comes an imperfect definition inherently tainted by its evolution. Language itself has history imbedded in it, evolving and developing alongside humanity. Language takes humanity's experiences and grows with them, developing the cancers of bias inherent to those experiences. Take a simple word as simple as "gun" and look inside to the emotions and biases that form within the gut, barring any personal experience with guns. It becomes difficult to form a dispassionate sentence or opinion simply because of the societal definition of the word, biases and all.

The inheritance of societal biases is true not only of language, but everything else within it. Objects, people, historical events, and all other phenomena that touch man are tainted. Besides the emotional stamps we place on phenomena through our own personal experiences, we also inherent the emotional stamps of society. We inculcate many of those ingrained biases, which ultimately come to affect our own behavior as they skew our thoughts and actions. Society's biases become our own, turning us into varying degrees of drones as we react in similar fashion to the common experiences of life. At the extremes of examples, abortions conjure up negative thoughts and feelings, and unthinkingly must be prohibited without consideration. On the other side, government charity conjures up pleasant thoughts and feelings, and also unthinkingly must be sought at any economic cost. Depending on the intensity of the emotional stamp, and thus the bias, as well as the level of self-awareness and free-spiritedness, each individual responds differently to his own biases, personal or societal. If no one considered the rational consequences of these built-in biases, we would wind up living in communist countries where charity is no longer a choice (and no longer charity, either), and where mothers were sacrificed for the sake of the baby.

The built-in danger of any norm or bias is its generalizing character. Not only do we imprison our own choices by blindly accepting a norm, we also run the risk of wrongly extrapolating to our own situations. No attitude, disposition, bias, or learned response pattern can be appropriate to all experiences. Every situation has its difference that changes the optimal response or reaction.

Although we cannot escape the built-in emotional stamps that accompany everything we know, we can think and choose despite them.

As much as we depend on society and society on us, neither take on characteristics that are always to the benefit of the other. Sometimes society benefits us, and sometimes we benefit society, and sometimes we act in ways that are detrimental to one another. At the heart of our actions are our own benefits. We do things because in the end we want something, even if simply to feel good. The impetuses behind our behaviors are our instincts, which have the success of the individual and his genes as their sole reasons for existence. And thus as a collection of individuals acting in their own benefit, we do things collectively that benefit the group because it indirectly benefits us, being that we are each part of that group. As part of the group, whatever benefits it benefits our individual selves. But along with those benefits might also be detriments borne unequally by the individual. For example, we could donate all our money to charity. Society in general benefits by our action, and as members of that society we benefit too. But, given that it was our money, we also lose out significantly. Just as we try to use our surroundings for our own growth and prosperity, so does society use individuals for its own growth and prosperity. Society, acting in what is in its best interest, would try to influence us into donating as much money as possible, without driving us into dependent bankruptcy. We, acting in our own best interest, would want to donate only as much as made us feel the best about ourselves and our financial state.

Our instincts usually wind up with the upper hand and protect us from doing things that are abnormally detrimental to our well being. But peer pressure, advertising, political posturing, governmental legislation, and lobbies are all powerful forms of societal influence. They are the post office of emotional stamping, trying to make us feel one way or another about the aspects of life. We should feel good by doing this, awful if we do that, buy this to belong, and donate that to be liked. Separating society's influence from our own personal experience, as well as from our rational expectations and our instinctual impulses, becomes confusing. But we need to be consciously aware of the behaviors and attitudes that society tries to impart on us to assess whether to incur them or not based on our own perspectives of our own best interests. In the end only we must live by the consequences of our actions, and we should base our decisions on those ultimate consequences and their desirability.

Since we live in a society, we must to some degree live by its rules, its languages, and its norms. Think that we could completely antagonize society and come to live independent of it would be naïve. We will always need the food, security, companionship, members of the opposite sex, and validation that society, to varying degrees, supplies us. If we completely lost the ability to relate and communicate with it, we would be doomed. Society has its purpose and its use, of which we should not lose sight. Anti-establishmentarianism for its own sake is no different from blind conformism, both trapping the person within the bounds of the credo.

We do not have the ability to choose nor change the ways society tries to influence us. We cannot get rid of the barrage of messages and biases that it imposes, nor the emotional stamping that come with it. We are a part of the world around us, and as we affect it, it affects us. But although we cannot change the biases, we can change their nature by the way we look at them, and feel about them. We can change the paradigms through which we interact with the world. It's a matter of going back to how we define things.

At the heart of our personal paradigm is our habit of labeling things as "good" or "bad." By placing these labels we unwittingly influence our future behavior. We want, seek, and encourage those things that are good, by definition of the word, thus binding our own behavior to the label and the definition. For example, we learn from society, especially one as consumeristic as ours, that pleasure is good and pain or sadness is bad. Happiness, laughter, and love are pleasurable things we should constantly seek. Sadness, pain, and loneliness are unpleasant and should be avoided. In time we become hedonists who go out and seek pleasure wherever we can find it, and avoid pain at all costs. And how can we blame ourselves? Pleasure and pain are our bodies' hot-wired carrot-and-stick incentives for getting us to behave the way that benefits our genes the most.

Labels exist for a reason. They allow us to shortcut redundant reasoning. Once we figure out that something is generally this or that, then labeling it as this or that saves us the time and energy of having to figure it out every time. But although not labeling is difficult, we neither have to accept the labels of others as our own, nor blindly accept our own labels in every circumstance. Pleasure is not always good, and pain is not always bad. For example, drugs are pleasurable, but hardcore use can lead to addiction and ultimately death. Unless the person's goals in life are to die young, then he would be doing himself a disservice by pursuing the pleasure of drugs at all costs. Similarly, exercise can be painful, but the benefits of exercise in all probability outweigh the pain.

Beyond simply being aware of labels and behaving despite them, there is greater power in instituting labels by choice and cognitive reason. We could suffer through the "bad" pain of exercise because we know it is good for us, or we could look forward to exercising and enjoy the "good" pain of exercise. Becoming a sort of masochist[26] does not happen overnight, but in time we can condition ourselves to like the experiences of exercise, pain and all. When that pain becomes equated with a better-looking body, with a healthier heart, with the reaching of milestones, we can come to like that pain for every reason we come to like the results of exercise. Feeling pain can come to mean feeling life, so exercise can become desirable. We've changed our outlook, switched labels, and therefore changed our behavior. These are all similar, but more cognitive forms, of positive emotional stamping.

Labels are also a source of societal manipulation through our conscience and accompanying emotional stamps. Although the formation of our conscience is in part influenced by our own instincts, society plays a large role through the formation of labels as discussed above. The conscience's function is mostly one of conscious influence of behavior through the imposition of emotional states according to the labels we have attached to behaviors. If we

---

[26] Masochism might have a bad connotation in your mind, but hopefully you are now letting go of the associated emotional stamps, biases, and labels to read with curiosity and not skepticism.

have labeled a certain behavior as "bad," then our conscience will instill in us a painful sense of guilt to influence us. If we have done something "good," then we feel pleasure.

If we are behaving unconsciously and merely acting according to our conscience, then we have objectivized ourselves and short-cut our own interests. The conscience has a use, but can also be easily misused. For example, many times our conscience dissuades us from doing something because it is against our own interest, but sometimes it dissuades us because it is against society's interest, according to our programmed labeling. We may be dissuaded by our conscience against rebelling against something because rebelling is "bad," but perhaps we sit on the sidelines of the American Revolution and rebelling would be in our own interest.

In order not to fall into the conscience's trap and instead regain our subjective selves, we need to raise our conscience to a conscious level and act not according to it, but according to its principles.

Sometimes we have to question what we feel according to our conscience and instead think of what is best according to what we want and believe. If we consciously act according to what we really believe, then we can nullify our conscience and its accompanying emotional stamps. Our conscience is a superficial guide that applies itself blind to circumstances. If we still feel leftover emotions such as guilt even after raising our conscience to a conscious level, then we have to wonder if we are only fooling ourselves into thinking we are doing what we believe is best. We might be able to fool ourselves consciously, but we cannot fool the subconscious.

Raising our awareness of our conscience might seem simple, but is difficult to put into regular practice given our strong inclination towards mental shortcuts. To stop ourselves and analyze a situation takes mental energy. Ignorance is bliss, and bliss is a powerful motivator. But just as mental laziness can be a habit, so can mental lucidity. With due practice, time, and work we can make a habit of stopping ourselves at the inflection points in life and reflect on the situations and our responses. But as difficult as is raising personal awareness, changing our underlying paradigms and labels is that much more so. Having grown up with our views, biases, and labels, retaining the status quo is easy and comforting. No work is involved in absorbing what we are taught, and then acting it back out, especially if we naturally seek validation. Through time, validation after validation only serves to reinforce all the biases and interpretations of society. Knowing that other people accept and agree with us, our decisions, and our behaviors, feels great. Validation would not work otherwise. But as important as validation is in ensuring that we do not become maladaptive and miserable, it is equally dangerous in tempting us into comforting conformism. There is a difference between validating our behavior with our surroundings, and giving into our surroundings. Literature and film, especially from the eighties teen genre, are rife with plots exemplifying the problems associated with validation-turned-conformism. *The Breakfast Club*, the quintessential brat-pack film, builds a story around the causes and effects of this conformism from the point of view of each distinct teenage stereotype of the time. Each character derived comfort from identifying and living within the attributed stereotype, relying on the easy validation that sprung from it. However, each character also displayed a latent desire to break away or rebel from the limitations of the stereotype. The rebel had a soft side he couldn't express, the princess had a lascivious side, the derelict had hidden beauty, etc. The characters bond during the movie as they explore their common desire to rebel from their comfortable stereotypes.

As was explained in the last section, we need validation to correct for our fallibility. We do commit mistakes, and we can't know everything. But that does not mean that society is always right. If true, we might as well be drones, for then what is the point of free choice? Free choice comes when we act despite our inclinations, despite external pressures, to do what is best rather than what is "right." We have the freedom to make rational choices, but that freedom is bought only through self-awareness. In order to make sound judgements we must be aware of all the different influences on our behavior.

We intrinsically and unavoidably know we need validation, but we have freedom over where and from whom we seek it, and in what ways. Seeking validation from those people we most respect and want to emulate would only make sense in relation to those facets of our lives from which they, in parallel, obtain the most respect. From our parents we might just want existential validation through love, from our bosses we might want validation of our careers, from our friends we might want moral validation. For example, if we acted out in a certain fashion and were told it was not appropriate by our friends, should we listen? Are our friends people we want to emulate morally? If our bosses told us certain actions were fine, should we listen? Seeking moral validation from our bosses would not make sense if we did not agree with their moral persuasions. Letting ourselves forget what it is about a person that we respect is easy, causing their influence over us in matters where they have no authority. Actors are typically used as political props because people blur the distinction between fame and political know-how. Why should we let ourselves be influenced by actors when it comes to politics?

Although that we should discriminate how we validate our behavior is seemingly obvious, we still fall trap to momentarily giving up our beliefs or principles to a figure of authority simply because of his position or because we respect his knowledge in one specific area. Just as easy is giving into peer pressure over things we originally did not want, and over matters in which our peers have no authority. The search for validation is a strong human trait, and it is thus important to actively discriminate over that search so we do not give up our will along the way. We must first acknowledge that we need validation, and then figure out what kind of validation is acceptable from whom, thus impeding the motivation to yield our will to others.

Chapter 3.

The Big Brother inside

Instinctual Influence

In earlier chapters we discussed the instincts' influence on behavior through emotional predispositioning We discussed how the instincts actively monitor what a person experiences and 1) taint that experience and the resulting response through the creation of emotions or feelings; 2) control how strongly an experience is stored in memory; or 3) outright hijack the brain into action in an emergency situation. This section will deal with the second tool of influence, the mechanism by which the instincts determine how strongly to store an experience into memory, and its practical significance.

To be worth noticing and remembering, events and experiences must be of some cognitive or psychological value to the individual, a value that is determined by the experiences' relation to the directives of the instincts. As these experiences impact an individual's ability to fulfill his instinctual needs, they take on "instinct-meaning" in direct correlation with the severity and extent of the impact. When things have either positive or negative value to the instincts, either as obstacles or as enablers of a need or directive, they become important in human terms. The instincts can prepare the mind and body to store an experience in memory with an appropriate amount of vividness and in the right context through the assignation of value.

In his book Fletcher only discusses cognitive value in terms of 'felt satisfaction', or in a positive sense, although it can also be applied in terms of threat, or in a negative sense, as was just indicated. Valuation in general is a mechanism by which different courses of action are all weighed against the same yardstick, regardless of whether responding to threats or seeking satisfaction,. In the end, we can only take one course of action at a time, and our minds must be judicious in choosing that course. Fletcher's arguments are in general agreement with this, implying that experience cognitively affects the individual according to its meaning, or value, in relation to the instincts:

> " 'Instinct-Meaning', in Lloyd Morgan's[27] view, is very closely related to the *affective* element in experience. Objects require meaning in terms of 'felt satisfaction'. These elements of satisfaction and dissatisfaction which play such a large part in the acquisition of 'meaning' are termed 'psychological values' . . . Then, considering the role of intelligence as being the modification of behavior in accordance with the psychological values, Lloyd Morgan goes on to distinguish intelligence on [different levels]."

The assigned value of an event, experience, phenomenon, object, or person is actively monitored and weighed by the instincts to determine the type and intensity of the emotional response, as well as the strength of the stored memory, in order to influence and signal "intelligence" on an appropriate course of action. Concentrating on immediate threats such as careening cars would be vital when walking along city streets, versus notic-

---

[27] Fletcher is reviewing C. Lloyd Morgan's book *The Interpretation of Nature*, Macmillan, 1905

ing clouds in the sky during particular situations. Our ability to concentrate on the threat is necessary for us to be able to respond to it. Something within us needs to direct us to focus on the threat and respond, otherwise we would be critically dysfunctional and would soon wind up dead because of an accident, in this case being run over by a car. The something that instructs us on where to aim our attention is instinct, and the mechanism used is valuation. The threat is more important to us because it carries more value than the cloud as per our immediate survival. The "role of intelligence" is to react to the threat, which has been deemed valuable. Our behavior is then modified according to that perceived value. The level of value perceived by the survival instinct indicates the intensity of the response, and thus the degree of impetus of behavior.

Although the instinctual assignation of value for the purposes of weighting the relevance and importance of empirical phenomena is universal, the method and manner of application varies greatly from person to person. Each person gets affected by objects and events in different ways depending on the physical characteristics of the person, on his experiences, his goals, and any other aspect of life that differentiates one person from the next. An athlete would place importance on any factors related to physical performance, while a religious person would place importance on spiritual issues. Knowledge of the variation in valuation systems is important because it is through a person's knowledge of himself, and what makes him unique, that he can know how to create value and feel self-worth. This seems obvious, but biases, blind spots, and laziness all obstruct a person's ability to create and pursue goals of worth and value. The world that exists in our minds is not an absolute world of objects and experiences, but a world of mental perceptions created by the mind according to its ability to sense the physical world and then interpret or convert that world into a mental one. This act of sensing and interpreting the physical world involves a system of highly subjective information filters and converters. This system of filters and converters allows us to focus on the significant things. Although the instincts provide the mechanism by which these filters and converters are created, the environment provides the context. If this environment is biased and insincere, then our filters and converters can become biased and insincere. We cannot pursue true value if bias blinds us to what it is and to the paths that lead to it. Our pursuit of value can either be hampered or focused by a system of information filters.

Blindness is born from the leeway we have in the interpretation of our surroundings. Although consciously deceiving ourselves is difficult, we do so unconsciously with everything we witness, interpreting things in ways that suit us, rather than in ways that would be deemed objective. Since the world is but the way our mind constructs it, our mind has leeway in how it places significance on events, and how it remembers them. Our mind receives sensory stimulus, and then matches it all together, along with historical events, to create a perception. When we see a train in one instant, then see it a few yards ahead the next, and then hear the sounds of horns, our minds put the information together to assume the train is moving and blaring its horn to inform people of its motion. The reality is that we could be moving and not the train, and that the horn actually came from a truck behind the train. But our mind constructs a story with the information it has, as best as it can. The information we receive is never complete and therefore our mind must fill the gaps with its own assumptions to make the story credible, and to allow us the freedom of acting based on the story we perceive. Of course our mind has substantial freedom in filling the gaps and making assumptions, and more often than not, those assumptions will be favorable to ourselves. When someone smiles in my direction and I feel good about myself at that moment from the transcribing of other previous events, I'm inclined to assume that they are smiling at me, and that they like me. In actuality, someone might be behind me and the person smiling does not even acknowledge my presence. The opposite could be true, as well. The

person could actually be smiling at me, but I assume it is someone behind me because I feel timid.

Figure 1. Illusion of a triangle within a
set of circles.

Another example of the mind's penchant towards filling information gaps are visual illusions. Figure 1 is a classical illusion
by which the human mind is tricked into seeing a triangle based
on the specific arrangement of three circles with a pie-shaped
piece removed. Although no distinct triangle with hard borders
exists, the mind fills in the missing border pieces to come up
with the triangular shape, assuming that the picture, and therefore the borders, are incomplete or missing.

The way we perceive events and phenomena is subjective.
How we assess and attribute value, and therefore what worth we
believe is to be had by life and the phenomena within it, is also
completely subjective. The values we place on events and phenomena depend on our disposition at any moment, on the view
we have of an event, on our role in it, on the information that is
missing, on the people involved, etc. All these variables play a
part on how our minds construct and perceive an event, on the
assumptions it makes to fill the gaps, and on the view it takes to
protect our egos.

The Freedom of Interpretation

Our personal valuation framework is difficult to change since it is based on internal programming and upbringing. Far easier than changing the overall framework is shifting its focus. As was discussed earlier regarding the reproductive instinct, we innately have a need to create and produce, a need built-in by instincts to induce us to have children. However, we do not necessarily need to have offspring to satisfy this innate need if we don't want to have children. We can instead shift its focus towards other forms of production such as marketable products or art, for example. We can fulfill a large number of the characteristics of the need for children through the production of other things; things that we can consider as our own creations, and that will help us achieve transcendence. What we cannot do, not easily anyway, is instead of shifting the focus, altogether ignore the need for engendering. To completely ignore a need and leave it unmet might leave us unsatisfied and empty. These needs are innate, instinctual, and strong. What we can hope to do is face them head on and try to satisfy them creatively rather than only through traditional means.

Being aware of our instinctual needs allows us to be cognizant of our valuation framework, our interpretations of our surroundings, and the effects of those interpretations upon us. Being aware allows us to shift and manipulate our valuation system to serve our needs, rather than it controlling us. Instead of blindly following the carrots and running from the sticks of instinctual influence, we can liberate ourselves through enlightened choices. Whereas before we had children to simply satisfy a "paternal/maternal" instinct, we can now create choice and instead choose among a plethora of ways to create as a response to an instinct to "engender."

Cognition of the valuation framework and the interpretive filter allows us to better choose our surroundings, our actions, and influence our interpretations to better suit us in terms of our

THE BIG BROTHER INSIDE

satisfaction, happiness, and fulfillment. We can choose the paths in our lives that will lead to the most personal value and shift the focus of the framework to one that best matches our environment and capabilities. If we know that our interpretation of things will also affect how we value them, then we can choose to interpret things in a light that will shed more value. The trick is not to deceive ourselves or be naïve, but to choose the interpretation that most suits us based on what we know about our personal valuation framework. Interpretation implies a range of choices, and we should choose the most rational choice that leads to the most benefit. It's tantamount to calling a glass half-full, where the glass is our framework, the liquid is the circumstance, and the choice of calling it half-full versus half-empty is the interpretation.

The role that interpretation plays takes on greater importance when we realize that the value we place on ourselves is in great part based on how we believe other people value us. As intrinsically social animals, we need to feel that society needs us as much, if not more, than we need society. This sense of value ensures that our behavior is tuned to the culture and society within which we live, a mechanism developed to monitor how well we interact with society.

We are dependent on those around us to give clues in determining what value we bring to society since we cannot determine it in isolation. Our subjective interpretation plays a role in first picking up the clues from our environment and the people within it, and then determining what those clues mean. It makes sense to choose an interpretation that is most beneficial, in a sense interpreting things again as half-full versus half-empty. I do not insinuate to pretend something is near-full when it's only half-full since that is simple self-deception, but adopting positive perspectives can have a domino effect in terms of increasing motivation and self-esteem.

A person's value must be imparted by others. Just as we cannot define a word by using that same word in the definition, we cannot derive value from that which we impart on ourselves. The value we impart on ourselves is self-reflective, and thus self-negating. For example, there would be no point in feeling wealthy by giving ourselves money. The value we add to society, the money given, is only as much as that which we give up in giving that money away to ourselves. The net effect is zero. However, if we gave money to a needy person, he would value the money more than we would since for him it would probably go toward satisfying his basic needs, while for us the money is more of a luxury. He values a marginal dime more than we do. The net value to society is positive since one man gained more than the other lost; society gained more through the needy person than it lost through us. This net gain in value is reflected back onto ourselves through various means—through the results of the act as well as the recognition of the act.

Recognition that imparts value need not be connected to the executor of the act. Anonymous acts still impart value as long as the consequences of the act are recognized. In the needy person's case, witnessing his satisfaction, hearing about it second hand, or even just imagining it is enough to impart significance. The mode of reflection of value is not important as long as the creation of it is external to the subject. This reflection then makes us feel valuable. Thus, as programmed and by definition, we depend on others to impart on us a sense of worth, even though the final value we perceive from others lies in our interpretations.

If we thought that any money given to the person would be completely wasted, then our interpretation of us, or anybody else, giving money to him would be negative. Although society might actually value charity as a whole, our bias would incite us to interpret society's reaction to charity negatively. In the end, all things must be filtered through our senses and interpretations. It thus makes sense to interpret things such that we derive the most from those interpretations, where all interpretations are assumed to be equally reasonable.

Fulfillment comes when we feel we have achieved the level of value to be worthy of life and the society within which we live. The goals we set in life should be based on how we can incrementally add value and feel recognized for it, whether internally or explicitly by others. The attainment of those goals will yield satisfaction. But one encompassing goal should exist at any point in time that will give the value to our lives that will allow us to feel like the life we lead is worth it, and that we will leave it having added more than we consumed. That goal varies according to the person and his age, be it raising successful children, a successful career, writing a successful novel, or whatever else people can create to derive value. Even taking on a hedonistic life imparts fulfilling value through pleasure and art, both of which, as can be seen by the size and importance of the media and entertainment industries, are valued in society. But fulfillment will only come by achieving the level of worth where we feel as though we have transcended our existence and died having left an impression. Although our instincts may always leave us wanting, our achievements should have an apex through which we feel we have ultimately fulfilled the hunger for life, reproduction, nurture, socialization, and any other manifestation of the instincts.

Stuck in a Search for Meaning

The preservation of life is inarguably one of the basic instincts, engendering in man a powerful will to live that affects practically everything he does. Although the instincts are hidden behind circumstances and environment, hidden along with the overlapping and intertwining of the instincts among themselves, all together they are the drivers of every action and thought. This mass of instincts, meshed together along with environmental forces, are abstractly known as the human will. The will to live, to die, to reproduce, and all others, together represent this larger will which breathes life and action into man.

Knowing our own will personally, and building an epistemology of the will as an aggregate race, brings us closer to the Socratic ideal of knowing and examining ourselves. Without this self-knowledge we become prisoners to the capriciousness of our wills, blowing in the wind of our own short-term needs and desires without satisfying any larger purposes. Both basic instincts are constantly creating a barrage of needs and desires that keep us on track in general and in response to our environments. We can easily become engrossed in the continuous act of putting out small instinctual fires without paying attention to the deeper recesses of our will.

The self-preservation instinct, much more than the instinct to reproduce, is in continuous fire-fighting mode and cannot be mollified for even a moment. With more difficulty we now stop and take account of the causes and effects of this continuous need for instinct satisfaction, since this need is constantly pawing at our attention.

What are the deeper behavioral justifications and ramifications of a constant need for survival? Physiologically and psychologically speaking, something at our core first creates this constant sense of need and then deals with its consequences. The natural reason for the unmitigable nature of the self-preservation instinct is that it is only useful when not mollified. The more intense the desire and passion to live, the higher the probability of survival, barring outright panic. This higher passion would incite a person to run a little faster from danger, to fight a little harder in defense of a threat, or to look a little closer for food. Waking up one morning and having a person or animal think that since he survived yesterday he is going to take a break today and not worry about it would not make any sense.

In previous chapters we described some of the physical and philosophical reasons behind man's desire. Scientists have actually made some headway in discovering the physiological processes behind desire, and tied it back to the instincts. As Melvin Konner[28] puts it,

> "[T]he motivational portions of the brain, particularly the hypothalamus, have functional characteristics relevant to the apparent chronicity of human dissatisfaction. Animal experiments on the lateral hypothalamus suggest . . . that the organism's chronic internal state will be a vague mixture of anxiety and desire-best described perhaps by the phrase 'I want,' spoken with or without an object for the verb."

The self-preservation instinct, manifested as desire in the above example, is not really satisfied or fulfilled when we attain a goal. An animal's, and a human's, internal physiology preempts satisfaction, and instead is continuously shifting the focus. Self-preservation is a continuous, ongoing thing, which cannot be satisfied at any one point in time. As long as we live, the self-preservation instinct will incite us to remain alive. Wealth does not incite us to feel that life has been vindicated and release the self-preservation instinct from its duty. In fact, becoming wealthy might strengthen the instinct by making us feel more valuable, and therefore make us feel that more is at stake.

One of the metaphysical manifestations, and psychological repercussions, of this continuous state of desire is what existentialists call the anguish of human particularity, or the anguish of the here and now. According to Olson, man is trapped within a limited portion of space and time, precluding him from knowing or obtaining things outside his local geography or moment in history. None of us participated in Ancient Roman culture, just as none of us will know what the twenty-fifth century will look like, just as none of us will ever own a teleportation device. All of us have a curiosity or desire to participate in geographies and times outside our influences, and our inability and powerlessness to do so engenders in us the anguish of human particu-

---

[28] As quoted by Csikszentmihalyi, pg. 31

larity. The manifestation of this anguish is a direct result of our overzealous nature to want and desire more than we can satiate.

As with the metaphysical derivation of the anguish of human particularity, other metaphysical manifestations of the instincts exist. Although impulses such as fight or flight are blatant physical manifestations of the self-preservation instinct, the underlying behavioral repercussions are more metaphysical than they are functional. The self-preservation works most of its magic beyond the perception of the conscious, its influence removed one or two levels from an action.

Our self-preservation instinct instills a passion for life to motivate us to preserve it. Metaphysically, we experience this passion as an anguish of being, an anguish engendered by our realization that being is as tenable as nothingness, that we will one day fall back into the nothingness from which we came. Functionally and of psychological consequence, that passion is the instinct's tool to manipulate us into working and fighting to live. We constantly save our own lives because we are inexorably pushed into it. But consequently, this must mean that to us our own life is worth preserving. We fight, we battle, and we work to secure those things necessary to preserve life because evolution has programmed a certain passion for life inside of us. Thus, rationally, we must be of the unconscious opinion that life is worth preserving.

Rationally, fighting for something that holds no value is pointless. We would not work and fight to save a single ant, for example, because that individual ant holds no value for us. We work and fight only for those things that have value, while we work and fight hardest for our own lives. Otherwise, logic would tell us that fighting and working to live would be pointless if life was worthless. Since we are naturally programmed to preserve our own and our relatives' lives with great passion, we must place an unexplainable value on those lives for which we feel so passionately.

We place this unexplainable, unconscious value to life, and

we are left, consciously, to ponder why. Humanity has been driven to ponder why. The rational answer, that life holds no value and that evolutionary necessity is the only reason for passion, is to most people objectionable and devoid of hope. This would mean that we do indeed feel a passion for life and a fear of death because we have been programmed to feel as such, without a justification for the feelings. Our lives are devoid of lasting worth and value, and we are mere automatons living out a fait written in our genes via our instincts. We are born, fight, and work to retain our lives for as long as we can, then we die, and the story begins again with our progeny. It is the most probable of all explanations of life, but it is also the bleakest and most difficult to swallow.

As thinking beings we strive to understand ourselves. We strive to understand what moves us, what makes us tick, why we behave the way we do. Our instincts are unconscious programming that we do not understand, but strive to. Where we cannot link a meaning to an emotion or a behavior, we rationalize a plausible answer. And our common answer to the inexplicable valuation of life is that it has a meaning beyond simple observation. To give us hope, we profess that life must have a hidden meaning, and that's why we value it and defend it instinctively.

But this presents a conundrum. Our rational disposition also leads us to conclude that life is meaningless. Like all other animals, we rise from the earth, make a brief appearance, and return to the earth. No mystery exists to a dispassionate and rational thinker. The appearance of life is simple, and seemingly unequivocal. Why, then, should the idea of life and death cause such a disturbance? Why must life have meaning? Irrationally, emotionally, human curiosity compels us to spend most of our lives in search of that hidden meaning. We search for that meaning because the rational reason, evolutionary manifestation, is too painful. Evolution has played its hand too efficiently and built in a sense of love and fear so strong that it's blinding. Our inherent fear of death, our love of life and people, our causal

valuation of life, all make it painful to acknowledge the temporality and the meaninglessness of our, of all humans', of all plants',
of all animals', existence. To acknowledge such would be seemingly self-defeating, and evolution has cruelly incarcerated us
within our emotions.

Our natural inclination toward self-preservation doesn't let
us go to bed at night with a rational state of mind. We must live
at all costs, we must preserve our ephemeral lives. Our lives must
have value, and thus they must have meaning. But since this
meaning is not self-evident, we conclude that that which we cannot explain logically, must be divine. In our abhorrence of a
knowledge vacuum, we turn to answers that are not of this world
or reality. If we cannot scientifically arrive at an answer, then we
make one up until we can prove otherwise. Our fear and hate of
ignorance is such that we would rather make up explanations
than leave something unsettled. Curiosity is a natural and inherent human, and animal, characteristic that is born from the need
to understand things so that we can preempt them, avoid them if
harmful, or seek them if useful. With knowledge comes the ability to master our environment and avoid surprises—both important to survival. With the constant development of new tools,
and the increasing availability of information and ease of communication, we have become in essence dependent on our ability to control and master our environment. When we find something that we cannot explain or understand, we become very
uncomfortable, to the point of creating hypothesis that we can
believe and upon which we can rely, regardless of proof. So
ingrained is this need for answers that when we cannot scientifically explain our behavior, we then turn to the metaphysical for
explanations; souls, spirits, and gods become the answers to our
behaviors and our environment. We do not understand our inherent valuation of life, so we explain it with meaning.

In the end, all of our actions lead back to the fulfillment of
our primal needs and instincts, of which some have developed
to secure not only our survival, but also our need for survival.

Developing the need for food would be pointless if we saw no point to living only to feed our hunger. We need to want to live to push ourselves to do so. This is true only of us, for we are the only animal with the ability to ponder existence. For animals who have no concept of life, it is not necessary to develop a need for it. Animals have their survival instincts to ensure their survival, as do we, but unfortunately for us, we have also developed the ability to question things, including our own existence. Our productivity and intelligence have furnished us with the most dangerous of luxuries, idle time. We are no longer completely busy trying to remain alive, but now have the time to question why we should bother to spend our time alive at all.

Unfortunately, at times philosophy has taken a backward step and bowed to the pressures of trying to find external meaning in existence, rather than focusing forward on defining and creating personal paths toward personal fulfillment. Some philosophers, and most religions, seek to lend a meaning to mitigate the emptiness and futility of life's struggles. In essence, they are filling man's need for a reason to live. Arguments have shifted toward the theoretical and metaphysical as answers to a baseless question since no other recourse is possible. To ask whether life has a meaning forces us out of our own reference point to an external one for judgment of our lives.

To give a meaning to something is to define that something and its effects within the broader confines of an external reference point. To give meaning to something is to acknowledge the value of it as more than just its immediate worth. I could give meaning to my own life, but that would be circular. Of course my life has meaning to me since I am wholly dependent and part of it. Everything that happens to my life impacts me, and thus has meaning to me.

One's life can have meaning only if someone or something else attributes a meaning to it. The first rational choices for that external attribution are personal relationships and society as a whole. As far as we impact those around us, and in some cases a whole society, we give those people the ability to give meaning to the effects we have had on their lives. We, in effect, can lend meaning to our lives by affecting those around us and offering them the opportunity to give meaning to our interactions. This meaning is real and tangible, but unfortunately, it is temporally bound to those we have had the opportunity to influence, and in most cases is bound to our lifetimes or those of our children and grandchildren. In some cases of fame and notoriety, such as the Einsteins and Alexander the Greats of society, the effects of their lives are very long lasting, and the meaning of their lives more endurable, but still bound by humanity's existence in the universe, and bound to human concepts.

In reality, although Alexander the Great's life impacted millions, and still impacts people today through cultural ramifications and historical accounts, as far as Alexander the Great is concerned, the meaning given to his life after his death is of no consequence to him. The meaning ascribed to his life was of consequence to Alexander only while he lived and could acknowledge it. In other words, it does not do Alexander any good now to be famous since he is not here to enjoy his fame. Being venerated today by millions does not make him any less dead. So in reality, the importance of the meaning of our lives is justified only while we live. Although that meaning can outlast us, and that potential transcendence is valuable to us while we exist, its importance to us only lasts while we do. In other words, the value of transcendence is only significant in terms of its potential, and not as actually achieved transcendence. Einstein probably felt incredible in knowing his legacy would outlive him, but that means nothing to him now. Things can only matter to us while we have the capability of assigning a worth to them. So that takes us back to a temporal meaning of life as it is defined within a societal framework to only the extent of our lives.

Although we should be happy with that, most of us are not. The anguish of being takes hold of us and it becomes painful to know that all that we know will essentially perish with us. While we live, we have the ability to assign a value and a meaning to everything around us. At the moment of our death, the world will cease to exist, and the beauty we found in it will die with us. The world will probably continue to exist after we die, and the beauty within it will probably continue to be appreciated by those that outlive us, but that means nothing to us. We know only that which we see, hear, feel, and in general, experience. The moment we lose the ability to acknowledge the presence of something and assign a value to it, is the moment that that something becomes worthless and ceases to exist.

A great world with great value will cease to exist, and that is an immense tragedy. That is immensely painful to know. But even worse is to know that we are among those things that will lose their value to us the moment we die, and at that moment our own lives will become worthless to us. The moment we perish, everything about us as only we know it, will perish, too. And that is a very painful fact to accept; to accept that all that happens now, all that has happened before, and all that will happen in the days to come, will become pointless and worthless with our deaths, because we will no longer exist to attribute a value to all those things.

Our neocortical brain has surpassed our subcortical brain in development, and the dissonances with which we are left are the aforementioned existential anguishes.

The Need for Transcendence

The most prominent manifestation of the evolutionary need for procreation is the development of a need for social transcendence. By social transcendence I mean our need of to feel as though we are more than that which spans our lifetime, worth more to society than what is physically left behind. We need to feel as though our essence will outlast our physical existence, correlating with our desire to procreate, and to become productive members of society. Whether the first is an emergent property of the latter two, or the latter two an intended consequence of the first, is difficult to tell. Regardless, having children offers both a way to achieve physical transcendence and interact positively with society. The value that we add is directly evinced through whatever actions our children take throughout their lifetimes, and past our own. As our children grow and take on attributes and goals independently, we feel we have added more to society than the sum of what we have contributed as parents since our children add value independent of our direct actions. Our children transcend their roles and assume the roles of productive members of society. Thus, in order to induce us to procreate and add lasting value to society, we have evolved a reproduction instinct that is evinced by the need for transcendental value.

Of course, this is not the only manifestation of the reproduction instinct. We also have sexual appetites and emotional needs, that along with the need for transcendental value and the pleasurable sensations created by the reproductive organs, provide a strong inducement toward procreation. Reproduction, and production in general, is so important, that evolution has built in an instinct along with physiological attributes to ensure that we procreate, and become productive members of society. But the manifested need for transcendental value, derived from the reproductive instinct, has the strongest and most far-reaching impact on the individual.

A philosophical consequence of the manifested need for social transcendence is our personification of society as an entity in and of itself with a higher purpose, elevating our own importance since we are a part of that anthropomorphic society. The society as an entity assumes its own higher reasons for being, be it to add intelligence and thus reason to the universe's existence, to add life to an otherwise cold universe, or whatever other higher purpose can be assigned. We not only have a need to assign meaning to our own existence, but as a part of society, develop a need to giving meaning to society as well. This identification with a collective society breeds the feeling of being more than merely an individual, of being a member of something bigger than the sum of its parts.

Another byproduct of this need for transcendence is the fulfillment of that need through means other than children, as was discussed earlier. Children are not the only way we can leave something behind, that can transcend existence, that can add value by more than what we produce. We can also create innovations, written materials, music, and so on, which take on a life of their own. A need for valuation creates the desire to add value to society, and the need for transcendence ensures that some of the value that we add will benefit not only current, but future, societies. The reproductive instinct might be better called the engendering instinct since it is not limited to procreation for satisfaction, but has other multiple outlets, all related to the engendering of something that transcends its creation, and its creator.

The good news is that there are multiple ways of feeling transcendent. The bad news is that it varies for each individual, and not knowing how to get there can be disastrous. We've all felt the emptiness that lies in the pit of our stomachs, some more intensely than others. It arises when we're most bored, with the least things to do, with the most disarray in our lives, with the least plans, without the faintest sense of direction. It is the same pit that arises when we lose a loved one or when we get fired. That pit of emptiness is the end-result of leaving our instincts dissatisfied, of losing our self-reflective sense of value, of leaving our need for transcendence unanswered. Without that way to escape our mortal selves, we fall into the terror of death and temporality, of meaninglessness and despair.

That risk of feeling the pit of emptiness is especially dire today, and becomes more so every decade. As technology improves and production rates increase, we are left with more and more idle time, and with more and more gratifying but unfulfilling luxuries of leisure. In times past the common man had to spend most of his waking time satisfying his basic instinctual needs—to work to secure food and necessities for himself and his family. Idle and leisure times hardly existed. By spending his time satisfying his instinctual needs he would have felt fulfilled at some base level because he was always serving his master, his instincts. They were satisfied, so he was satisfied.

Now that we have been afforded more leisure and idle time than work time, our instincts need higher, more abstract levels of satisfaction. Rather than merely physically satisfying our instinctual needs, we now have to metaphysically satisfy them. In the end our instincts are the driving force of life, and we are ultimately and incessantly alive to satisfy them. But the focus has shifted from subsistence to existential.

What have we done now that we have all this extra time on our hands, time that was originally spent subsisting? First we have expanded the definition of subsistence so that practically everything becomes life-or-death in importance (is there a more histrionic culture than the American?), thereby seemingly satiating our primal instincts. Then we turned everything else into symbols and metaphors for subsistence and procreation so that we are still indirectly satiating our instincts. Kids *need* every toy and candy they see, women *need* every article of clothing they want, and men *need* every gadget and tool they have. But when that is not enough, they acquire cars as an extension and show of their virility, as a cliché example.

Having idle time has another risk attached—thought. Idle time affords us the ability to think and hypothesize, to daydream and fantasize. We start viewing our existence in larger contexts, and begin to desire more, becoming uncomfortable with our current states. Thought, both our savior and our scourge, has become a double-edged sword whose second edge was sharpened by the first. It was through innovation that man discovered idle time, and at once took on an absurd existence. The true paradox is that as meaningless and miserable as is idle time, we are all endlessly working and searching for it.

Transparent Meaning

Even though the Socratic ideal of living a self-reflective and examined life is worthy, it is difficult, too. Biases are blinding, and therefore hard to root out in ourselves. Regardless of the difficulty, though, an examined life is still the only one worth living, and the results worth the effort. Living the Socratic ideal involves looking a little deeper behind our principle, ideals, and choices, to root out the underlying assumptions. Although living a *completely* examined life is counterproductive, after all our inherent mental laziness came about for a reason, examination still serves a valuable purpose in certain situations—whenever we have to make an important decision, or whenever we feel that we are making a decision because we'd rather *not* do the opposite, rather than because we *want* to engage in the action. In other words, we're better off investigating the assumptions behind a decision when we're acting out of bad faith, be it spite, revenge, hate, etc. By acting in bad faith we are most likely choosing a course of action that is sub-optimal simply because we are not doing what we *really* want to do, but rather what we have rationalized to do. By making our assumptions transparent we open ourselves to the whole gamut of possibilities, rather than just those that have passed through our mental filters.

Our search for meaning is also a bias. We start to judge phenomena based on the extrinsic meaning of those phenomena in relation to us. We begin to take actions and make decisions if they can add meaning. As with any other bias, we become prisoners to our searches for meaning, excluding choices that are otherwise rational. As Nietzsche tells us, we begin to tolerate and excuse suffering, because it has meaning.

Believing that life and everything in it has meaning is not inherently bad or wrong. In fact, believing that everything has great meaning can be uplifting, just as believing that life has meaning and then failing to find it can be depressing. But life is not usually a bed of roses, and the latter, the disappointment, usually accompanies the former, the uplift, in time. Through knowledge of the underlying assumptions of the search for meaning a person at least has the choice of getting off the roller coaster, or become privy to a new set of freedoms.

Tracking the unconscious rationalizations of the instinctual will, the underlying assumptions to meaning are that life holds value because we find ourselves defending it vehemently. Determining whether life in fact holds intrinsic value is impossible since it all depends on the definition of value and the reference points taken. What kind of value, and in relation to what? But striking out this assumption of meaning altogether and implying that life holds no intrinsic value, we are lead to implicitly acknowledge that, like other animals, we are living out our evolutionary programming. In essence, all living beings then simply become instinct-realizing phenomena, and all phenomena and objects become tools in our personal search for instinct-realization. To some this is crude and apprehensible, to others it's natural and simple.

For those who choose an instinct-realizing assumption, reconciling the emptiness of life is difficult except by filling it with the joy afforded by nature. Life becomes a matter of squeezing the lemonade out of the lemon while some remains. All the work involved in squeezing the lemon then has a point—to get the lemonade. Life's struggles become pointless for their own sake, but they become important when they yield the juice of enjoyment, satisfaction, and fulfillment. Through the recognition and realization of death comes an affirmation of life. Through consciousness of freedom flows meaning, since being-in-itself comes to light through the realization of death and we understand the emptiness and pointlessness of life when we deny ourselves choice. Regardless of the assumptions we hold, making them should be an option based in freedom.

Chapter 4.

The Emotional Animal

Intelligence and Freedom

Knowledge and intelligence are necessary components of freedom. In Chapter One we discussed how freedom depends upon our ability to create choices through the conception of other states of being, and through our ability to project our selves. The greater our knowledge of other possibilities, the more choices we engender, the more freedom we have. We discussed how freedom is not an effect of the absence of obstacles but rather of the existence of obstacles to overcome. The more knowledgeable and intelligent we are, the more we can envisage obstacles and the manners of overcoming them. Freedom is absent in situations where we confront insurmountable obstacles. In that case they become limitations. A jail is only a jail as long as it is inescapable, physically or mentally.

In order to understand our limitations to freedom, we must understand the limitations and power of our own intelligence. What is the basis of our intelligence, and thus what is the basis of our freedom? The more effective we are at conceptualization and at the use of our own intelligence, the better we can maneuver through life.

This and the following chapters explore intelligence, starting with an analysis of emotions and intellectualization. As will be seen, emotions play a larger role in our ability to comprehend ourselves and our circumstances, and therefore deserve more credit and attention in thinking and decision making. Since freedom lies not only in the conceptualization of choices, but also in their analysis, intelligence becomes an important and necessary component.

We can either be captive to our emotions, by failing to heed their implied messages or conversely by only acting out intuitively, or we can use them as a higher order of intelligence. Within emotions lies the power of motivation, and we can either fall prey to those motivations, or use them to our own advantage.

Physiological Theories on Emotions

Contemporarily, much work has gone into understanding human emotions. As was explained earlier, Dr. Damasio divides emotions into primary and secondary. Primary emotions are the innate reactions by the limbic system, which short circuit the neocortex in order to preempt it. Those emotions are purely reflexive, and thus are the way the instincts taint an experience to influence the response, and to influence future behavior.

As discussed, the primary emotions start with the perception of sensorial stimuli, which are intercepted by the amygdala. The amygdala gets the stimuli before the neocortex, then by influencing the limbic system, alters the state of the body. The coordinated activity of the limbic system releases hormones, chemicals, and neural signals that alter superficial composure, the gastrointestinal system, the vascular system, and the neurological system among many others, to holistically profile an emotion.

These coordinated somatic profiles are what create shivers down our backs, butterflies in our stomachs, and emptiness in our chests. The brain senses all these changes and forms a perception of the somatic state, which along with a comparison of the previous somatic state, comprises the sensation of an emotion. Fear, for example, might be defined by activation of the dermis through cold sweat, activation of the gastrointestinal system through increased secretion of digestive juices and ensuing stomach butterflies, activation of the vascular system through increased heart rate, and so on. The sensation of all these things together profiles the emotion of fear. This act of sensing a somatic state, and the changes in somatic states, Dr. Damasio calls "feeling."

The neocortex also induces secondary emotions. Two different types of secondary emotions exist, depending on the desired intensity and timing of the emotion. The first is a somatically induced secondary emotion, which is generally more intense, longer to activate, and longer lasting. This type of emotion, through the work of the limbic system, induces the body state that first originated it. Thus the brain actually feels the emotion since it is reproduced in the brain and body through physiological means. The difference between the original and the recalled emotion is that the recalled emotion is initiated by the neocortex, instead of being reflexively induced to external stimuli by the limbic system, and its intensity might vary according to the strength of the memory or the experience that recalled it. With the induced secondary emotion the body actually changes states, and the brain and body feel and interpret it.

The second type of secondary emotion is merely perceived. The limbic system does not actually change body states, but instead fires off the stored image of the emotion to mimic its perception. This allows for a faster response, and perhaps saves emotional and physical energy. Regardless, instead of feeling the emotion throughout the brain and body, the brain instead duplicates the neurological processes and images that gave rise to the original emotion, thus allowing the mind to sense the emotion without actually feeling it. Without this ability we would become merciless prisoners of our emotions, given the amount of information and memory recall we go through each day. Our bodies would be constantly going through states of fear, anguish, apprehension, and elation, among many other emotional states, which would be incredibly taxing.

Behavioral Implications of Emotions

Contemporary thinking divides intelligence into two categories, intellectual and emotional (some frameworks divide intelligence even further, into eight or more categories)[29]. Intellectual intelligence is associated with memorization, recall, logic, mathematics, and spatial visualization, while emotional intelligence is more often associated with communication, intuition, and creativity. I would broaden and in a sense depart from this definition of the categorizations of intelligence. The two different types of intelligence cannot be divided so easily.

As discussed earlier, words can have a linguistic definition, and an emotional definition. A piece of artwork, for example, can be intellectualized into facts such as artist, mood, perspective, medium, etc., without any creative association. A piece of art that holds no relevance to its audience can be stored in memory through a linguistic medium, and thus be analyzed using intellectual intelligence. Just because its artist may have used creativity in producing the artwork does not mean that it must be analyzed by its audience through emotional intelligence. However, that same piece of artwork could remind its audience of an experience, aesthetic or other, and be associated and thus stored via emotional means, and thus analyzed using emotional intelligence.

The difference between the two types of intelligence lies in the method by which the individual stores, recalls, and associates a concept. An intellectually intelligent individual is adept at

---

[29] Goldman, pgs. 36-39

storing, recalling, and linking facts together without emotional attachment. He's great at trivia and at making logical jumps between facts. On the other hand, an emotionally intelligent individual is adept at finding personal relevance to concepts, and at storing, recalling, and linking concepts together using experiences and emotions. He would be more adept at associating and linking where those links are unforeseeable or seemingly illogical, yet valid.

The intellectual would go from A to D by first knowing that A links to B which links to C which links to D. On the other hand, the emotionally intelligent individual would know that A links to D because somewhere in his experiences he's seen it and thus now intuits it to be so, but can't explain why. He can skip B and C, making the connection between A and D seem illogical at first, but in the end valid nonetheless because experience is his teacher and proof, and emotions and experience his link.

A genius would be adept at both types of intelligence. Albert Einstein, the German-born U.S. physicist of unparalleled global fame for his genius, would intuit the end result of his theories first, and then go back and make the logical case. He dubbed true intelligence as imagination, or as I would call it, emotional intelligence. But then again, he also had the luxury of possessing the intellectual intelligence to back up his imagination. In the world of science, and in most other fields, few things mean much unless they are either provable or recreatable. Yet I still would have to agree with Einstein, since abstraction is only possible using emotional intelligence, and emotional intelligence is that which separates us from today's and tomorrow's artificial intelligence. That's not to say that the intellectual is not intelligent, but more often than not it will be the emotional one who will make the leaps in the fields of knowledge and creativity because he is not bounded by logic and sequence. If C were missing, the intellectual would never get to D, while the emotional man would. Naturally, we are neither strictly intellectual nor emotional. We all must learn language and logic to communicate, and we all have emotions and relevant experiences, but our aptitudes in using the two vary.

But emotional interpretation is not perfect since emotions and experiences carry baggage. Emotions can be tied to memories, or can trigger other emotions or states of being. As such, abstract concepts can then be irrelevantly linked to experiences or physical states that confuse the definition of the concept. But amazingly enough the mind's normal transference of emotions onto words or concepts is mild enough that any attached baggage becomes imperceptible, especially if it is irrelevant.

The Power of Emotions

Instinct and human knowledge are intimately connected. Instinct not only monitors and influences the experiences upon which we build knowledge, it also determines the way that knowledge is perceived, categorized, stored, and recalled. As was explained in previous chapters, instincts use emotions as one of their main tools in influencing behavior and affecting knowledge. This use of emotions by the instincts, however, has a significant corollary effect, which is the human ability of abstraction.

Abstraction is divided into two basic types, linguistic and conceptual. Linguistic or symbolic abstraction, that discussed in the section "The Role of Language," is the ability to generalize and aggregate parts into a symbolic whole, such as the abstraction of all animals that meow, purr, have vertical slits for pupils, are agile, have four legs, and so on, as cats. When it comes to linguistic abstraction, the human mind is very limited in its ability to conceptualize the literal meanings; it is limited in the number of parameters or parts it can handle simultaneously, and in the number of links it can envision. These mental limits pose physical boundaries around how well linguistic abstractions can be understood.

For example, man's conceptualization of the abstract concept of "the human body" is very limited. In general we understand that a human body is normally made up of two legs, two arms, a torso, etc. But to understand at a deeper level all the different organ systems and their interactions is difficult. Even though the human body encapsulates both levels of abstraction, the mind can only comprehend the more superficial one. Yes, the human body is a collection of torso, arms, legs, and the like, but then, what is an arm? Then, what is a bicep? Then, what is muscle? This reduction could continue ad absurdium, only to prove that words are nothing but symbols. Although we can give the body a name, this does not mean that we truly understand its meaning. For example, because of this limited understanding, man will never completely comprehend the effects any drug has on the human body because of the number and complexity of all the interacting systems therein. But by breaking down the body into smaller subsystems, man can make strong estimates based on focused experimentation. Doctors study all the subsystems separately, the gastrointestinal system, the skeletal system, the circulatory system, and so on, and through experience can draw tables of known diseases, problems, and drug interactions. They can even study some of the links between the systems, but they will be severely limited in how many systems they can master, and in how many links they can envisage. As such, they might know what effects a certain drug tends to have on a certain system in certain circumstances, but they will never be able to explain the effects of that drug on all the systems, and the ensuing repercussions of all those effects on any one system. A doctor will never be able to tell you what effect a drug has on the human "body," but he will be able to approximate the effects on some of its subsystems. Too many systems interact in too many ways for any man to ever conceptualize. So we will forever be limited to drawing probability tables and creating computer models of interactions based on experimentation. Man thus can abstract the human body symbolically to be able talk about it holistically, but his literal understanding remains superficial.

As the brain and the body are intimately connected to give rise to the human mind, its workings are also something we cannot currently, and may never be able to, fully understand. We cannot understand the mind because we cannot understand the underlying physiology of the brain and body much deeper than their linguistic abstractions. A certain poetry exists in man's inability to understand himself. It is ironic that the package that creates something as powerful as cognizant intelligence has itself become so complicated that the intelligence to which it gives rise cannot comprehend how it does it.

Even though we cannot understand them literally, we can still understand them conceptually. Without the symbolic reductio ad absurdium, we can still grasp the terms body, brain, and mind, through the use of a second type of abstraction, that derived from the use of emotions by the instincts. That second type is conceptual abstraction, or the understanding of things other than through sensorial data or linguistic definition. At the highest end of conceptual abstraction are those things that defy sensorial or linguistic definition, concepts such as nothingness or love.

Concepts need not defy linguistic or sensorial definition to be understood abstractly. In fact, most, if not all, concepts contain some sort of conceptual abstraction[30]. Recent neuroscientific advances regarding human emotions and the advancement of modern philosophy together help explain this in more detail.

Martin Heidegger, the German philosopher of the early twentieth century, made a brilliant breakthrough when he equated his concept of nothingness to "dread." As he aptly explained, it is impossible for human minds to conceive of a definition for the

---

[30] As Hayakawa explains, the same could be said of linguistic abstraction since all that man knows he knows through symbols. Man does not directly know what any phenomena or objects are in themselves since he is bound to experience them indirectly through his senses. Thus, all human knowledge is known through symbols such as names, and thus through linguistic or symbolic abstraction. The name is not the object and the object is not the name; the name simply points to the object.

concept of nothingness. The minute we try to define nothing-ness, we are making it into something. A definition by nature objectifies that which it defines. Once nothingness is objecti-fied, it becomes something, that which the definition explains. However, we all still "understand" nothingness. Heidegger wrote about it, and he had faith that we would understand what he meant by it. Nothingness is an abstract concept that although impossible to define or capture with words, is still somehow com-prehensible.

To Heidegger the concept of nothingness was the feeling of dread. Incapable of attaching words to the concept, Heidegger's mind attached feelings. Instead of defining it linguistically, he defined it emotionally. At some point in his life the word or con-cept of nothingness was introduced, and at that point he or the people around him probably conveyed dread, and he attached that feeling to the word. From that moment on, Heidegger de-fined the concept of nothingness as the feeling of dread. I have to admit that the idea instantly clicked with me because I too define nothingness with that same feeling of dread. Perhaps it is because I dread non-existence, and therefore nothingness. But whatever the emotional definition, lacking the ability to use words, our minds turn to emotions to define the abstract.

As was explained in Chapter Two, all experiences come at-tached with emotions. The amygdala contains a short circuit that allows it to respond emotionally to a situation about the same time the neocortex has developed a response to the situa-tion, allowing the brain to store the situation, and the response, with an accompanying emotion or feeling. The response by the neocortex might also involve the inducement of a secondary emotion based on recalled experiences, which can also be stored as part of the current experience. This secondary emotion could provide the link between the new concept and the part of the experience that induced a recalled emotional reaction. The new word or concept now has a primary emotion to define it, along with a secondary emotion that links it to associated experiences and concepts from the past[31]. Words and concepts that are learned more by experience and context than by other words (which is how most words are learned) have the accompanying emotions or feelings that the experience emoted to define them. Thus, instincts can not only attach an emotion to an experience to influence behavior, they also attach an emotion to words and concepts to influence the way we structure thought and communicate.

This mechanism of learning yields the higher power of the human mind. Language is only one form of mental conceptualization, emotions being another more advanced form. Language is limiting by its structure, rules of utilization, strict definitions, etc. Not only that, the number of words readily available for use in conversation is limited. We have all been frustrated by not being able to find or remember the right word to convey an idea or concept. Emotions, on the other hand, have no such limitations. They are only limited by degrees and types. Emotionally abstract concepts are abstract because they defy linguistic interpretation. This type of abstraction is not conceptualized with language, but with feelings and emotions.

Of course, abstraction exists in varying levels, with nothingness at the extreme, and the concept of life somewhere at the lower end. We can define life, give it words and ideas to match. But because we can define it linguistically does not mean that we cannot define it emotionally and abstractly. We all understand the concept of life as it is told in the dictionary, but we also personally understand it as the sum of our experiences and emotions. Life has a different abstract meaning depending on personal experiences. We can explain life through words such as

---

[31] Dr. Damasio developed a similar theory, but on a broader scale. The theory, dubbed the "somatic marker hypothesis" by Dr. Damasio, states that all experiences, options, and concepts are marked by a somatic state, which depending on the state, bias the mind for or against that experience, option, or concept. The more negatively marked an option, the more likely the mind is to discount it consciously or unconsciously when evaluating options. Thus emotions play a role in rational and analytical thinking.

reproduction and growth, and others will comprehend the meaning. But the word will be of no importance until its relevance to the listener is unearthed. Therein lies the power of higher intelligence. To take a word without definition such as nothingness, and make it comprehendible, relevant, and alive through an emotional association. Now we have the power to think at a higher plane not afforded through mere linguistic interpretation or definition. We can now imagine things that had never been seen and could never be defined merely through emotional transference.

Chapter 5.

Free Choice and
Non-deterministic Behavior

Determinism and Behaviorism

What the will and the consciousness have in common—
and basically what all organisms on Earth have in common—is
that at the most basic level we are all reactive beings. Every impulse we have, every thought we form, and every word we utter
can be traced back to a stimulus, be it internal or external, to
which we are reacting. We eat (at least some of the time) because we are internally stimulated by hunger; we laugh because
we are externally stimulated by a comical situation. Even the
complex task of planning a vacation is a response to various
different possible circumstances. Those circumstances range from
the simple request for a vacation by a spouse to an internal need
for rest caused by stress to the arrival of a holiday. Regardless, we
plan the vacation because of an occurrence or situation: We are
invited, we need rest, or we have free time. We don't plan vaca-

tions simply because we can; rather, we plan them because something incited us to do it. This is true of absolutely everything we do: We do things as responses to stimuli. Sometimes discovering what the stimulus was proves difficult, but tracing back actions or thought patterns will eventually lead us to it.

The notion that the mind is essentially a reactive system is not new. The concept, championed as behaviorism by John B. Watson early in the twentieth century, and by many of the behaviorists who followed, argued that all human action is performed purely as a reaction to external stimuli and that any triggered response was originally developed as a learned reflex. The reactions merely mirror the witnessed responses. Thus, they contended, concepts such as consciousness had no formal use. Instead, they stipulated, all man needs to do to understand and predict his own behavior is observe and study himself.

Behaviorists later added the idea of conditional reflexes to their theories. They contended that the mind not only mirrors its learned response patterns, but that it also learns from the environment's responses to the individual's reactions in order to fine-tune future reactions. In other words, the mind learns which responses are favorable and which aren't based on the punishments and rewards doled out by the environment. The more rewards a certain reaction receives, the more that reaction becomes ingrained.

Modern social psychology has evinced that though behaviorist theory applies to a limited degree, the mind is vastly more complex than early behaviorists envisioned. Social psychologists poked holes in behaviorist theories by studying human behavior that is unexplainable through pure behaviorist rationale.

For example, Elliott Aronson's landmark social psychology book, *The Social Animal*, discusses how, in isolated incidences, receiving substantial rewards for performing an act or duty induces little or no behavioral change in a subject compared to performing the same act or duty with small remuneration. Aronson reasoned that the smaller the remuneration, the more the subject has to adjust his attitude and behavior to justify the action. In other words, if I hated spinach, but someone paid me 1,000 dollars to eat a plate of it, I would have no problem doing so. The money would be ample justification for my eating spinach even though I hated it. However, if someone paid me one dollar to eat spinach and I agreed, it does not quite justify putting myself through the trouble of eating a plateful of spinach. To justify compromising myself for one dollar, I would have to convince myself that I really thought spinach was good. Either I would think of myself as a cheapskate for eating things I didn't like for one dollar, or I would convince myself that I made an easy dollar by eating something I did not mind eating. The latter is far easier on the ego, and as Aronson strongly suggests, one of the highest priorities of the mind is ego protection. The human mind is constantly defending and reinforcing the ego to maintain and increase courage and self-esteem.

In short, behaviorist theory in principle is correct, but not quite as early behaviorists envisioned. Its application is probably far more complex (I say probably because little is known with certainty about the operation of the human mind) than envisioned. As modern psychologists have come to realize, the mind probably contains elements of many of the different theories, from Darwinian instincts to behavioral reflex. The mind does have the capabilities of sensing time lapse, prognostication, and imagination, whether the capabilities come about through a recurrent network or other functional system. Regardless, behaviorism simply cannot account for those mental capabilities.

Early behaviorists wished to discount consciousness, but the existence of instincts and the unpredictability of human behavior necessitates the conscious as a concept to structure the complexities of the human mind, especially including the mind's ability of self-awareness. Pure reflexive and conditional reaction theories are not enough to explain complex human interaction. A *priori* instincts play a part in how humans interact, and thus discredit pure behaviorist theory. However, modern psychology needs to, and by and large does, incorporate a form of behaviorism in explaining human behavior.

While Darwinism and evolutionary psychology explain the innate motivations behind much of human behavior, behaviorism helps explain some of the effects of experience on mental development, and the pre-Freudian concepts of the will and consciousness help encapsulate and structure the complex interaction between instincts and experience. Although the Freudian concepts of the ego, the id, and the superego are helpful in compartmentalizing the mind and its functions for the sake of pathological psychoanalysis, this structure is too burdensome as a tool toward understanding the mechanisms and development of human behavior.

It is important to understand that concepts such as will, consciousness, and ego, are all human constructs and models aimed at providing a structure by which to understand the complex processes and functions of the mind. They are not necessarily the physical way the mind is compartmentalized or structured, but are ways to describe its characteristics, to model its processes and interaction with the external world. Being descriptive and categorical, these concepts are not provable, but some are more effective than others as tools aimed at understanding ourselves and how we think. They should thus be judged by their usefulness and applicability more than anything else.

Multithreaded Consciousness

In this book I partly digress from popular psychological concepts which partition consciousness into conscious, subconscious, and unconscious types. Although I do use those terms in this book to encapsulate variances in mental activity, actually dividing the mind into these categories gives the illusion that the brain is also partitioned according to mental activity types[32]. Current neuroscientific theory evinces the error that such a framework founds.

Dr. Damasio explains in his book that the classical homunculus theory, which is the theory that the brain has a centralized CPU (Central Processing Unit) or "little man" to coordinate and compile information, and the classical Cartesian Theater theory, which is that the brain compiles all sensory information in one region of the brain, are demonstrably wrong. Instead, the brain is comprised of multiple regions and centers that are interconnected through jungles of nerves, fibers, and synapses. At any point in time multiple number of regions or centers are receiving, sending, and processing information. The sensory regions are receiving and interpreting information from the senses, the subcortical regions are receiving and sending homeostatic information regarding somatic states, the motor cortex is moving the body in response to stimulus, and so on. All these interactions, and many more, are all going on at the same time in different areas of the brain.

The activity in one area of the brain influences the activity in another through the fibers connecting the areas both directly and indirectly, but no central CPU exists to coordinate and compile the information from all the regions in the brain. If such an area existed, we would see brain damage cases with that CPU area of the brain debilitated, henceforth impacting the activity of all the other regions. But such cases do not exist, and in their stead are cases where people lose control of parts of their bodies, or they lose the ability to use a sensory organ, or they lose a specific component of what is considered normal, rational behavior. But damage to the individual processing areas of the brain never causes overall loss of activity by the brain. Since the brain regions can, and do, function relatively independently, damaging one area affects only the responding mental function that

---

[32] Mental activity types are not to be confused with brain functions. Although no region in the brain is dedicated to subconscious thought, the brain does contain regions dedicated to understanding language.

area serves, and impairs the interdependent functions. In fact neuroanatomists map the regions of the brain to mental functions, and basically learn about the brain by studying brain-damage cases. They map the area damaged and observe the ensuing impairment in activity.

The homunculus theory of the brain was the basis for the classical conception of consciousness. Previous theory assumed that the brain had a CPU that processed information so that relevant information was passed on to the conscious, while the rest was acted upon automatically and unconsciously. In effect, the brain had a second brain inside it. This theory was very convenient in the way it explained the complexity inherent in the brain, as well as how well it fit modern philosophical and psychological theory, but lack of empirical support has made it lose favor. In its stead is a new time-dependent theory.

The new neuroscientific theory of the mind is that the brain is processing different information in its multiple regions at all times, and along with those multiple regions are also multiple centers of convergence. While these centers compile information with high interdependence, no one center puts it all together. Instead, the information dispersed throughout the brain is connected by timing. Since all the regions of the brain are interconnected directly through fibers, or indirectly through intermediate regions or chemicals and hormones in the body, synchronicity is what coordinates the information lying therein. Two, or how many dozens of thoughts occur at any one point in time, interact simply by the fact they occur synchronously. The sensory systems affect the motor systems, which affect the homeostatic systems by virtue that they are connected physically and chronologically. At any one point in time we are releasing hormones and chemicals into the body to regulate its activities, we are breathing and our hearts are beating, we are adjusting our posture to retain balance, we are blinking our eyes, we are listening for abnormal sounds, feeling external temperature throughout our bodies, and concentrating on the task at hand. We are doing dozens of activities that are considered normal functioning, but are aware of only one or two at any point in time.

In fact, according to Paul M. Churchland professor of philosophy at the University of California, San Diego, neurophysiologists have discovered that the brain has a background neural activity frequency of forty hertz. In other words, the brain seems to function at an oscillatory speed of forty cycles per second, an oscillatory speed present throughout all brain regions, keeping them in synchronicity. A part of the brain is seemingly in charge of generating pulses of energy from which the rest of the brain functions, pulses timed at forty hertz. We would think that if that part of the brain was damaged, the rest would not be able to function, as if we had "pulled the plug." According to Churchland, that is exactly what happens. The intralaminar nucleus of the thalamus is credited with the task, and in cases where such nucleus is damaged bilaterally (to both sides of the brain), the person in effect goes into an irrecoverable coma. This might seem to contradict my earlier denouncement of the homunculus theory, but it does not. What is damaged is not a central processing center, but the power cord that gives the brain the timed energy bursts to function.

With all this said, can we then say that it is only the task at hand of which we are conscious, and everything else is subconscious, unconscious, or automatic? No, we cannot. Thinking back to a few seconds ago, we could probably remember what we heard, felt, or saw in our periphery, although at the time we were unaware of it all. We were not conscious of the bird that flew out of the corner of our eye the moment we saw it, but if someone asked us about it later, we probably could remember it. We did not perceive the bird "unconsciously" or "subconsciously" because when prompted we can recall it as though at the time we were actually conscious of it. And to an extent, we were. We are actually conscious of everything that we feel, sense, and think at any one point in time, but at different levels.

No line separates consciousness from subconsciousness or unconsciousness, instead we have levels of consciousness. In order to focus, we can only be aware of one, two, or three things at any point in time, even though the brain is processing multitudes of things. We are only strongly aware of the most important and relevant mental images, while the rest occur in a state of semi-awareness. The most important images are the most conscious, while the most repetitive, automatic, or irrelevant are the ones of which we are least conscious.

If we are listening to classical music and reading at the same time, eventually the music fades into the background and we become only mildly aware of it. Reading assumes primary importance, and we become most aware and conscious of it. However, if the music station suddenly switched to playing heavy metal rock, the change would make the audible system the most important and we would become most conscious of it. We would stop reading and concentrate on listening, if even for a moment. We always listened and interpreted what we heard, but were barely conscious of it. If asked to what we were listening, chances are we would be able to recreate parts of the song and answer the question. Only when a change in music occurred did we become most aware to what we were listening.

Since consciousness exists in levels, we are in effect conscious of everything that we do that we can sense or feel, even if the level were so low we would hardly be able to remember it. The only things that are truly unconscious or subconscious are those things that our minds regulate that our brains are not privy to feeling or sensing directly, such as the controlled release of chemicals and hormones, or the regulation of the immune system. As to those things we can directly feel or sense, our minds are continuously processing them with scant awareness from us, but with just as much, if not more, rigor. If we start falling forward, for example, our brains decide to stick out an arm and a foot to regain balance. Our brains made a decision on which body parts to move, how much, and how quickly. The process was so quick and reflexive that we became aware of it only after it occurred by experiencing the repercussions of the movements. We were never fully conscious of losing balance, and we were never fully conscious of the decision to move our bodies in response. But it happened anyway.

Our minds work at many different levels and on many different things at the same time, but we are only fully aware of the most important and relevant. Thus separating the mind into consciousness, subconsciousness, and unconsciousness is severely limiting the actual power and dynamism of the mind. Although they are useful terms for the grouping of consciousness levels, it is important to remember that the division lines are arbitrarily applied and the groupings do not actually describe different brain functions. The terms subconscious and unconscious are still useful as a way to describe those things of which we are barely aware, but no clear line separates those things of which we are fully aware from those of which we are partially aware, from those we are not aware of at all.

As has been argued, consciousness comprises far more than that for which we have given it credit. In fact, it gets far more convoluted than to which this book alludes. In her book, Patricia Churchland references groups of studies involving patients that underwent commissurotomy to introduce another discontinuity in the traditional understanding of the conscious self. Commissurotomy involves splitting the two hemispheres of the brain by cutting the largest set of connecting fibers, called the corpus callosum, for medical reasons. The procedure, first practiced on animals and then on humans, had striking effects. Patricia Churchland describes one such experiment:

> "In one experimental setup, visual information is sent exclusively to one hemisphere and then a question

is posed to see whether the information is available to the other hemisphere. For example, the subject fixates on a midpoint, and a tachistoscope[33] is used to flash a signal to one visual hemifield for a designated period . . . If the word 'spoon' is flashed to the right hemisphere, and the subject is asked to report what he saw, he answers 'nothing,' but if he is asked to use his left hand to feel under the cloth for the object seen, the left hand picks out a spoon."

What the studies thus demonstrated was that the two hemispheres learned and acted independently and *without knowledge* of each other. In other words, one side of the brain could be given information privy to only itself, and then respond only within its range of possibilities, always without the knowledge of the other. Similarly, one hemisphere would be taught a task without the knowledge of the other and then perform that task, also without the latter's knowledge. In the experiments the brain performs as if two virtual brains coexisted in one physical one, each completely unaware of the other.

As Patricia Churchland puts it:

"One is accustomed to thinking of oneself as a single, unified, coherent *self.* The possibility that underlying that customary conception is something diverse and divisible, something whose coherence may be tied to coherence of input and output or to anatomical connectedness, rather than to an 'intrinsic coherence of selfness,' is the possibility ushered in by the split-brain studies. At first blush it is a startling possibility."

Thus the traditional understanding of consciousness is dealt another blow. Just as consciousness can no longer be considered an integration of distinct parts (conscious, subconscious, and unconscious), consciousness can no longer be considered a

---

[33] A tachistoscope is an experimental instrument that splits images sent to the eyes such that they are only displayed to one of the two hemispheres.

whole at all. In its stead is a collection of divisible systems working in unison, privy to different inputs and outputs, at varying levels of cognizance. We can no longer think of ourselves as a holistic self broken down into functional components subservient to the whole, but as a collection of independent components that when connected together make up the impression of a whole.

The notion of the self is an engineered illusion, the same as, as some have argued, the mind itself. The notion of the mind denotes a single, holistic, metaphysical concept that is independent of its physical roots. Its processes were traditionally beyond human comprehension and thus grouped into a single concept. However, we are slowly beginning to chip away at the mystery of the human brain, bringing the metaphysical mind a bit closer to earth. No longer can the mind and brain be seen as separate and independent in light of the results of surgical procedures such as commissurotomies and lobotomies, or in the light of non-invasive mental profiling techniques such as positron emission tomographies (PET) or functional magnetic resonance (FMR). Physically influencing the brain influences the function of the mind, and vice versa. They are intimately connected, and we are only beginning to understand how.

Building Neural Models

Through the modeling of the human mind according to models we can come to understand the basis of freedom. This basis lies in man's ability to perceive multiple options in response to a situation, to be able to choose among those options and focus his attention, and then to influence his mind and body toward a goal. Similarly, and as will be discussed in future sections, freedom also lies in our abilities to detach ourselves from our senses of self to be able to constantly redefine them. By understanding brain function better we can let go of our conceptualizations of the self according to metaphysical models and paradigms.

Research into Artificial Intelligence and neural network models has yielded a number of breakthroughs in man's understanding of the brain and how it functions. As was discussed in the last section, the traditional homunculus theory of the brain no longer fits our understanding of consciousness and its multifunctional capacities. In technical jargon, the traditional theory represented a serial processing system typical to desktop computers, with the homunculus being the CPU. As with desktops, we thought the brain handled one thing at a time while creating the illusion of handling multiple things through its speed and time-division capabilities. But essentially, serial processing meant central control over the system, handling things in sequence.

According to Paul Churchland, contemporary theory instead envisions the mind working as a parallel distributed processing (PDP) network, the time-dependent system described in the previous section. What this means is that instead of processing things sequentially, as a PDP network the brain can process and compare patterns and vectors simultaneously through multiple processing centers. In neuroscientific terms those centers may be cortical regions, subcortical nuclei, or other neural systems. As a PDP network the brain can receive intensity patterns and compare them to the intensity patterns stored in memory. Examples of intensity patterns are the visual outline of a fruit or the taste vector of a fruit[34], made up of degrees of sweetness, bitterness, sourness, and saltiness. Working in conjunction, the visual center and the taste center can, through linguistic association, come up with the name of the fruit.

Science envisions neural recognition in the following way. When a sense organ receives a signal, be it light on the eye or a flavor on the tongue, it is translated into an electrochemical signal in the receptor cells of the brain that replicate the pattern and intensity of the original one. This intensity pattern is recorded in a group of cells within the brain, which become the target cells for that one, specific, intensity pattern, the visual figure or taste vector. This pattern is recorded in the target cells through electrochemical firing potentials. When this pattern is fired off again in the sense organ, it travels through the relevant parts of the brain, activating the specific group of target cells that match this pattern. This tells the brain that the pattern has been seen before and is now recognized. The level of recognition depends on how closely the two patterns match. Studies in animals have shown that the activation patterns in the visual cortex topographically match the visual pattern the animal is seeing[35]. Scientists could recognize what the animal saw by looking at the cell activation pattern in the animal's brain.

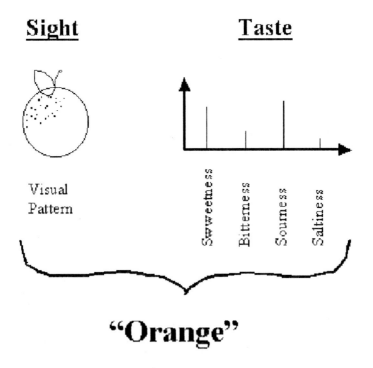

Figure 2. Neural representations of an ornage

---

[34] Note that the representational vectors can also be time sequential, such as a song or the movement of throwing a ball.

The processing centers in a PDP network, whatever they may ultimately be, are not dependent upon each other, which allows for fault tolerance. Fault tolerance means that if a part of a center errs or shuts down, the center as a whole can still function, or if a whole center errs or shuts down, the other centers also can still continue working. This is evident in stroke patients who lose a portion of their brains, yet can still function outside of the specialized capability of that portion. For example, the condition called aphasia is produced by the death of a specific region in the brain, either by stroke or through lesions, whereby patients lose the ability to speak. However, they can still understand language in general[36], and can in fact still function almost perfectly in every other way.

I say "almost," however, because the centers are still connected to each other in some fashion. Thus if one center goes down, the others are affected according to how they relate. For example if I lose the ability to process sound, then the other parts of the brain involving language will be affected, and perhaps even my ability to remember sound. Although I can still function more or less in society, I will suffer some impairment in related capabilities.

Churchland goes on to further breakdown brain function, such as the ability to think into the future, according to neural models, adding more and more complexity to the models. But the principal point remains—yes, I am because I think, but that "I" is no longer that which thinks. What I perceive to think is only a small subsection of all the thoughts in my head; any one ability or function of thought is dispensable to it because of the brain's fault-tolerance; and intangible thoughts are manifestations of physical events.

---

[35] Damasio, pg. 104

Synthesizing Theories on the Mind

To help put it all together, let us envision the human mind as a standing domino arrangement. The dominos are arranged in various patterns, some standing next to many different ones that start multiple chains, some acting as a converging point to multiple chains, and some ending a chain. They will just stay at rest until something nudges the first domino enough for it to fall. Without that nudge, they will not move. But once that first one is nudged, it will start a chain falling one after the other. Similarly, concepts, memories, ideas, and perceptions in our brains are linked together in patterns so that one thought will trigger another one by association, which will trigger another one, and so on, as envisaged by Descarte in *Meditations*. These associations are links between thoughts, the links that would make us think of coffee at the mention of café, which might make us think of hot, which might make us think of burn, which might make us think of ointment, and so on. The triggering stops when either the associations end (similar to the domino chain ending with the last domino in the chain), a stronger chain gets started with a new stimulus that disrupts the first, or the chain simply fades out slowly.

For example, let us say we see a dirty car on the street. That causes us to think about the state of our cars by association, which reminds us that they too are dirty, which causes us to plan to have them cleaned that evening, which reminds us of our dinner plans for that evening, and so on. In isolation, we have no idea why we called our friends to discuss dinner, but tracing our thoughts back we see that we did it through a chain of internal responses to the car on the street. Each thought in the series of thoughts is akin to a domino in a chain. As they are linked by physical proximity, thoughts are linked by association, be it physical characteristics, phonetic similarity, circumstantial similarities, and so on.

As Csikszentmihalyi states, the brain and its chains of thought

---

[36] Damasio, pg. 20

can become so long that they become essentially independent of the origins of their electrochemical impulses. Although this is only true to a point since the brain does need some sort of impetus to begin the domino chain, the mind can thereafter internally influence its own thoughts and actions, forming feed-forward and feedback loops.

Our brains, and all its domino chains, have been molded and patterned based on both our experiences and our genetic instincts. Based on the experiences we have had with cars, our response to the sight of a particular car will vary from person to person. Perhaps we owned similar cars and will therefore perform internal comparisons and feel pride or envy. Or perhaps we were once hit by similar cars so our responses are to move away from the curb. Whatever the responses, they are partly related to our experiences with cars in general. Our experiences laid the links between concepts so that a stimulus would automatically lead to associated responses partly determined by the past. In other words, if we were once hit by a Volvo, then that memory would be imprinted in our minds, and we might associate Volvos with pain. The next time we saw a Volvo, barring other experiences, we would follow the association to pain, which would cause us, among a range of other possibilities, to move away from the curb in fright. Responses, whether physical or mental, can always be traced back to an originating stimulus.

However, experience is only partially responsible for laying the domino chains. The other inputs that shape our responses are our innate instincts. In the example of a Volvo racing towards us, threatening to run us over, experience alone would not necessarily cause us to jump toward the curb out of fear. We could have done nothing, started crying, jumped away, attacked the car, or an infinite number of other things. Regardless, we all would have had our self-preservation instincts kick in to some degree as responses to threats. We may be able to learn to jump away from cars given the sight of one approaching us, but we cannot learn from observation to induce our bodies to shoot adrenaline and hormones into the blood stream as a response to a car approaching rapidly. The sympathetic response from the human body to spur it to action is innate and instinctual. However, whether we think the approaching car is a threat or not, and thus whether it induces a sympathetic response or not, can be learned, or unlearned. But the instinctual sympathetic response to fear will influence our behaviors and actions.

To help clarify the role instincts play in the development of behavior, let us construct a hypothetical situation. Let us imagine a family of pioneers moving into the American West, never having seen bears before. Now let us imagine that three brothers from this family go foraging into the woods for food. These three brothers confront two bears. One of them, far away from the situation, witnesses the first freeze in fright, while the second runs in panic. The brother who freezes gets ignored by the bear, while the one who panicked is attacked and killed. With this situation in mind, what would we assume the witnessing brother's reaction to be when faced with the same situation a week later? Although he saw both situations, we would rightfully assume that he would mimic the situation most likely to save his life, even though neither response independently should prove to be a stronger domino chain among his response patterns. He now has two choices to act out based on his experiences with bears, and everything else being equal, neither one should be a stronger learned response over the other. But we would know that that would not be the case; the brother would choose, consciously or unconsciously, the option most likely to save his life. The two developed domino chains are not equal in strength, although a behaviorist theory would assume that they would be. In other words, we have a built-in, instinctually mandated bias to do things that preserve our own lives in response to our environment, in this case learning to respond to bears.

What internal process places different weights on the two hypothetical domino chains? The answer, to recap Chapter Two, has something to do with the way the instincts influence the way an experience is remembered. The instincts capture an experience and stamp it with an emotion, prioritize it according to the instincts' directives of survival and reproduction, then store the experience and the learned response according to its priority. Neurologically, that priority may be derived according to the strength of synaptic connections (or through another undiscovered means). In terms of network models, the priority might be assigned through a predisposition toward a pattern or vector, or through the preactivation of a pattern. Metaphorically, I will describe the strength by the proximity of the dominos in the chain.

Thus, in the example of the brothers and the bears, the self-preservation instinct will place priority on the learned response that increases the our chance of survival, which is to freeze when confronted by a bear. That response is stronger because it is associated with a positive emotion incurred as a reaction to seeing the threatened brother survive, and it is stronger because the heightened sense of elation from his survival imparted vividness to the memory. But where does the sympathetic response to the threat fit in? The sympathetic response is an automatic and unconscious response by the amygdala triggered preemptively by the perception of a threat. At the sight of a bear near him, the last brother would sense a threat, and his subcortical brain would act automatically and unconsciously with a sympathetic response, as was discussed in Chapter Two.

What the brother does with the unleashed energy of the sympathetic response depends upon his learned response patterns and the strength of those patterns. But the subcortical response by the brain to induce the body into action occurs regardless of cortical reasoning. The autonomic responses, such as the sympathetic response, lie outside the cortical domino chain. The mind learns to perceive and interpret threats by experience, but the sympathetic response, once triggered by this learning, occurs automatically and outside the control of cortical thought. The response is not a choice but a reflex that occurs concomitantly with the brother's choice of action, whether to remain still or hide and flee. Regardless, he'll feel a surge of energy, an energy to which he must give some kind of outlet.

The subcortical response is akin to the human hand that starts the domino chain in the first place. Depending on the emotional setting placed by the amygdala, the first domino either gets a slight nudge to get it in motion, or a strong push, giving preference to certain chains over other ones. Along the way, the subcortical hand continually nudges and pushes certain chains to give them preference over other ones through the invocation of emotions, and through degrees of sympathetic, parasympathetic, or other autonomic responses.

In the above example, at the threat of a bear looking at him, the brother has a number of possible responses, including responses to other stimuli such as a bird flying overhead at that same moment. But the emotion of fear, the sympathetic response, and all the other subcortical reflexes to a threat, kick in. Those reflexes are akin to a hand pushing the first domino in the direction of the fight-or-flight response, and the continuous invocation of those reflexive responses are akin to the hand continually nudging the domino chains that belong to the fight-or-flight response, while dampening or stopping all the other ones. The subcortical brain cannot create or remove chains other than those it was either born with or derived through experience, but it can nudge certain ones and dampen or stop others as they are forced into motion.

The reality of behavior is that instincts usually play a subtle role. The differences in strength between responses, and the gravity of the situation, is not usually life threatening. The responses induced are usually not as extreme as in the example of the brothers. They may subtly affect what or whom we find attractive, to what we plan to do with our lives. Instincts influence the formation and strength of domino chains and their overall patterns. But because they are created both from the influence of experience *and* instinct, separating those out is impossible.

Overall how we adapt the instincts to ourselves will vary from person to person, but the instincts' existence is universal, whatever form they take. And the manifestation of the instincts will vary from person to person, but their effect on response patterns is also universal. The existence of instincts are as characteristic as the possession of opposable thumbs. We acquired those characteristics through evolution because they helped us at one point, in one way or another, successfully reproduce and survive.

Chaotic Human Behavior

Our needs, although influenced by and developed according to our surroundings and experiences, are essentially rooted in our instinctual nature. As we have seen, our instincts influence our actions in multiple, complex ways. These channels or ways of influence help determine experiences, which in turn structure thought patterns, which, along with the instincts, again help determine experiences. The loop continues throughout life.

Our power over our instincts and source of freedom from a deterministic life lie in that we can understand our instincts and learn from our experiences to help influence future ones. We can, in effect, alter and influence the development chain through built-in feedback and feed-forward mechanisms. By choosing the future environments in which we will place ourselves, and by actively channeling our wills, we are determining the types of people we wish to be, because our chosen experiences will then help shape who we are from then on.

Influencing our own growth and development is powerful. We not only can choose the environments in which we wish to place ourselves for the sake of the immediate experiences, but also for the sake of future influence. By environment I mean the people, the city, the neighborhood, the friends, the jobs, the recreational activities, and all the other things that we can choose to include in our lives. For example, we typically tend to take on the traits and habits of friends and loved ones, both out of respect and habit formation. By actively choosing the people with which we spend most of our time we are actively choosing what kinds of traits and habits we wish to assume.

But choosing an environment is the milder way of influencing our own future behavior. More powerful is the ability to channel our instincts and wills toward more desirable ends. All actions are performed as a mix of responses to external stimuli and manifestations of instincts. Choosing environments and experiences influences the first type of action—response to external stimulus—since the instigator of the stimulus has been chosen. On the other hand, channeling instincts influences the second type of action—instinctual manifestation, or acting based on an instinctual impulse. I will explain this phenomenon in greater detail in Chapter Six, but our capacities to influence the execution of our instinctual wills lie in the fact that instincts can be manifested and enacted in numerous ways, and an individual has a subtle choice in those manifestations and executions. As the sociologist Ronald Fletcher[37] puts it:

> " . . . whilst maintaining that the instincts are not in themselves learned, McDougall[38] lays emphasis upon the fact that certain features of the instincts can be modified by learning . . . to a considerable degree in the higher animals and man. Thus, by the associations resulting from experience, the *perception* exciting the instinctive behavior can be modified, and, by the learning of alternative modes of action, the *motor-activity* involved in the instinctive behavior can be modified."

Although we cannot change the behavioral guidelines instituted by the instincts, we can change the inputs that trigger them (the *perceptions*), and the resulting output (the *motor-activity*,

---

[37] Ronald Fletcher, pg. 101
[38] William McDougall, *An Introduction to Social Psychology*, 29th Edition, Methuen, 1948

or enacted behavior). In the example of the brothers and the bears, the remaining brothers have, and can continue to, modify their behaviors relating to bears through experience and learning.

Chapter 6.

Know Thyself

Will, Idea, and Consciousness

Arthur Schopenhauer, the renowned nineteenth-century German philosopher, had theorized that human existence could be divided into two components, will and idea. By idea Schopenhauer meant that the existence known to the individual was purely a function of his mind, a perception. Everything, including physical objects, the body, even a person's conscious self, all existed to the individual as mental interpretations or images, as ideas. Everything known to the individual exists as a mental concept, regardless of its form, and regardless of its absolute or transcendental existence. An object is known by how the mind perceives it from within the human brain, at a physical distance from the object itself. The mind will never really know what or how it is to be the object itself, but will only know the object through its characteristics that together make the perception, or idea, of the object. For example, we may see a table and get to know the table by its physical appearance, smell, taste, and touch, but we will not know what it feels like to be a table. We will not know what it means to be a table.

While Schopenhauer's notion of idea is existence as is known to us through the interpretation and creation of mental perceptions, the conscious mind, in contrast, is the mental function by which the world as idea is *formed*. The conscious mind is the faculty that interprets and creates perceptions of the world, while consciousness is the dynamic version of Schopenhauer's idea: it is the time-dependent existence of the world as idea. Consciousness is the total existence of all the coterminous perceptions or ideas of an individual in a point in time as they are related to the self by the individual. My conscious existence is made up of all the things I perceive as I relate them to myself given a moment in time. As will be discussed later, cognizant consciousness implies awareness of the self, and the relating of phenomena to the self.

Although Schopenhauer had a passive view of consciousness, Sartre had a more modern and dynamic one. Sartre had theorized that consciousness is consciousness of something. It can only exist in the presence of stimuli of which to be conscious. Without objects to see, sounds to hear, sensations to feel, thoughts and dreams to imagine, consciousness cannot form perceptions and the will cannot react. In essence, without stimulus, the mind experiences nothingness.

To be conscious, we need to be responding to something, or to be observant or conscious of something. Consciousness cannot exist in a vacuum. That is why sensory deprivation drives the human mind toward insanity. Without stimulation to seed thought, the mind can only remember and think about memorized events for so long before it would have to turn to delusions to maintain consciousness. Without an external reference point, those delusions would become reality[39]. Since consciousness is consciousness of objects and phenomena, it depends on those

---

[39] *The Oxford Companion to the Mind* states "[Sensory deprivation subject have] a strong tendency to develop hallucinations and hallucinogenic drug-like experiences not altogether dissimilar from those of schizophrenia... suggesting that fairly continuous inputs are required to maintain the sensory system in calibration."

objects and phenomena for existence. Without them, consciousness threatens to collapse into itself; to become nothingness.

The final component of Schopenhauer's model of the mind is the will. The will is that part of the mind that generates the mental impulses to act. To Schopenhauer, the will comprises all the innate and developed human impulses such as jealousy, desire, anger, and sympathy, and it also comprises all the other forces of actions such as the reflexes and the Pavlovian conditional response mechanisms. In effect, the will is the force that gives the mind the motivation to act. As Schopenhauer puts it, the will is the nugget of existence. It is the cause of interaction between the subject, or the individual, and the world as he perceives it. The conscious mindputs all stimuli together into a perception, and the will impels the individual to respond to it.

Consciousness of the Will

In getting to know ourselves and the manifestation of the innate instincts within us, we need to observe our reactions to different situations as casual observers would. What form, and to what degree, are we jealous? What do we value, and therefore for what are we desirous? We can answer those questions only by observation.

To understand ourselves, we must observe and analyze our responses and our impulses as if we were observing another person. Our continuous impulses are internal responses that we cannot control to come into or out of existence. Whether or not we feel an impulse of jealousy or anger is not up to us; i.e., how we intuitively react internally to something is not under our control. However, how that internal impulse gets acted out *is* up to us. How we manifest our will is under our control. Whether we act on our feelings and carry through our intuitive response is up to us.

The conscious mind plays the part of analytical observer,

and also actor. To understand what it means to be conscious of the will, we need to step back and understand the relationship between consciousness and existence. Edmund Husserl, the German philosopher famous for his development of the theory of phenomenology, theorized that consciousness precedes existence, or in other words, that we and other objects "exist" because we are conscious of the fact that they exist. Something does not exist until we acknowledge or have an intention towards it. The existence we talk about here is a subject-dependent perspective, championed by nineteenth-century philosophers and twentieth-century quantum physicists.

This relativistic view of the world according to philosophers takes the individual as an independent being lacking the capacity to confirm or verify his perceptions. In other words, because we are fallible and trapped within a fallible body, we cannot trust anything to be true for sure, and therefore we cannot prove anything for absolute. Existence can only be known relative to the self.

In the world of physics, certain quantum phenomena seem to depend on the state of the observer vis-à-vis the experiment[40]. As the observer changes the way he views the experiment, the results of the experiment differ to reflect the change. This poses many problems currently boggling physicists, but a possible explanation is that reality is indeed subject-dependent.

What must be understood is that the term "existence" is a human conception, and therefore bound to human consciousness. Husserl was not implying that humans breath existence to objects in an absolute sense by observing them (although some quantum theories state exactly this of subject-dependent phenomena). It's not necessarily the case that the moment we go to sleep the world ceases to exist.

Of those things that we cannot observe past, present, or future we will have no knowledge and therefore their existence is indeterminable and irrelevant. Existence, a concept of human creation, is known only to us as it relates to ourselves, our lives,

---

[40] Gribbin, *Schroedinger's Kittens*, Chapter Four

and our experiences, and are therefore unknowable beyond the realm of consciousness. The existences we know and of which we are conscious are the only ones as far as our lives are concerned, and therefore the only existences that should or can concern us. We cannot perceive, conceive of, or verify an absolute reality or existence, and therefore cannot have any meaningful relation to it. Things might exist absolutely, but as humans we will never be able to conceive of it or prove it.

Something exists *as far as we know* only because we are conscious of it. If objects do not intersect our perceptions then they do not exist to us, and therefore do not exist at all because we know of nothing external to the "to us," or to the subjective. Consciousness therefore precedes existence since consciousness is a necessary condition of existence. If we died tomorrow everything would cease to exist to us. Whether things continued to exist absolutely is irrelevant because there is no foundation for anybody or anything to verify the absolute existence of anything. As long as we are dead we cannot acknowledge the existence of things and therefore all things cease to exist, with the understanding that existence is a self-reflective human invention. Following this line of thought, consciousness also precedes our own existence, or in other words, in order to exist, we ourselves must be aware of our own existence. Since our minds can be divided into will and consciousness, then it follows that consciousness of our own existence means consciousness of both our wills and our own consciousness.

Consciousness of consciousness is de facto, while consciousness of the will is done through observation. In other words, to be conscious necessarily *implies* the former state since it involves observation and analysis of phenomena as they occur in relation to the self. We are conscious because we can observe things as they relate to us, that "us" being our conscious selves. There is no need to prove or show consciousness of consciousness because by definition, consciousness is conscious of itself. A dog is not conscious in the cognizant sense of the word, as opposed to the sense of the word that merely implies working mental faculties, because a dog does not relate phenomena to itself. A dog will chase its own tail because it does not have a sense of self on which to attach its tail. The tail is just a tail to be chased, it does not understand the tail as belonging to itself. Respectively, humans are conscious because they relate phenomena to themselves. People do not try to communicate with a mirror because they understand that the image in the mirror is their own, that the image is a reflection of the self. So in order *to be* conscious, we must be aware *of* our consciousness since it means relating phenomena with respect to itself, which means that consciousness of the mind is de facto.

Consciousness of the will, however, comes about through the witnessing of it, as if we were observing someone else. We only know our wills as much as we observe them, just as we only get to know other people through witnessing them. We don't know our wills until they compel us to act. However, once they do, we observe them and provide feedback to tune how our wills will further incite us to act. For instance, if we saw our mates with people of the opposite gender, we would impulsively feel jealous. Depending on the circumstances and our inclination towards jealousy, our wills would incite a gamut of responses, from violent action to passive observance. We would immediately start to act toward the aim our wills incited us to, whatever it may be. But immediately after our initial responses—say our blood pressures rose, our adrenaline kicked in, and our faces became flush with blood, our consciousness' would view these initial responses and weigh them against the circumstances, such as who the other people might be, how large they were, who was around, and so on. Our consciousness' might, for example, realize that the people were just acquaintances and feed that back to our wills, at which point we would react by calming down and switching our attentions to weightier matters. We thus are not necessarily prisoners to our wills, but administrators of them.

Freedom through Understanding of the Will

As was seen in the previous section, consciousness precedes existence, which means that we give existence to the will only through our observation of it. As we observe it and give it existence, we also separate it from the self. Observation implies a subject (that observes), and an object (which is observed.) The will, being the object, is separate from the self, the observing subject. We thus, through observation or consciousness, transcend the will and exist despite it[41]. We, in essence, gain a degree of freedom from it. But this is only possible as far and as long as we are conscious of it. Through consciousness, our wills become a part of the physical persona from which we are independent, from which we can free ourselves.

To take a step back, I do not want to intimate that the will and instincts are interchangeable. The will is another human abstraction and model, while the instincts are physically encapsulated phenomena. One can partly describe the will as being comprised of the impetus of the instincts, along with the accompanying structural responses. We are incited into an action by the will according to the energy given off by the instincts, and the motor action mostly described by experience (some motor responses are instinctual in themselves). We can internally and mentally "observe" our wills, but we cannot observe an instinct in any form since it is derived according to the structure of the neurological system. Looking at a bunch of neurons tells us about as much about our instincts as looking at a motherboard tells us about an operating system. But the closest we can come to knowing and understanding our instincts is through our knowledge of our will.

We can learn about our innate instincts by observing how our wills react to situations. We can learn about ourselves as we would other people; by observing patterns. Just as we would change our behaviors toward people based on what we know

---

[41] Instances in which our will, or our limbic system, hijacks our mind is an exception, but even then there are things we can do to try and preclude and free ourselves from them

about them, we need to adapt our own behaviors toward our wills. We need to learn about our needs and instincts so we can tune our behaviors and focus our energy in the manners that we deem most suitable, be it seeking happiness, fulfillment, or whatever other states of being we pursue. Our abilities to perceive are what yield intelligence, while our wills are the driving energy behind life. We must use one to understand and focus the other.

Only by understanding our will can we increase our freedom from its control. As Goleman explains:

> "At its best, self-observation allows just such an equanimous awareness of passionate or turbulent feelings. At a minimum, it manifests itself simply as a slight stepping back from experience, a parallel stream of consciousness that is "meta"; hovering above or beside the main flow, aware of what is happening rather than being immersed and lost in it. It is the difference between, for example, being murderously enraged at someone and having the self-reflexive thought "This is anger I'm feeling" even as you are enraged. In terms of the neural mechanics of awareness, this subtle shift in mental activity presumably signals that neocortical circuits are actively monitoring the emotion, a first step in gaining some control. This awareness of emotions is the fundamental emotional competence on which others, such as emotional self-control, build."

By practicing self-awareness and observing and monitoring the will, an individual is in a better position to dampen the effects of the subcortical impulses, along with the accompanying motor responses, on several grounds. First, physiologically, being self-aware decreases the amygdala's chances of hijacking control of the brain through a series of self-perpetuating responses. For example, anger can breed violence, which breeds aggression and more anger, which breeds more violence, which then reinforces the feedback loop to more anger, aggressiveness, and violence, until the individual reaches the point at which the amygdala can completely take control of the brain as a reaction to a perceived emergency.

Goleman narrates the story of a convicted murderer who panics when a burglary he attempts goes sour when the victim sees his face and threatens to reveal him to the police. The would-be burglar panics and kills the witness/ victim without perceived control of his actions. He later states that he has no idea what came over him.

> "Such emotional explosions are neural hijackings. At those moments, evidence suggests, a center in the limbic brain proclaims an emergency, recruiting the rest of the brain to its urgent agenda. The hijacking occurs in an instant, triggering this reaction crucial moments before the neocortex, the thinking brain, has had a chance to glimpse fully what is happening, let alone decide if it is a good idea. The hallmark of such a hijack is that once the moment passes, those so possessed have the sense of not knowing what came over them."

The idea of the neural hijacking is espoused by the "insanity plea" in American courtrooms. Goleman's arguments could be seen as supporting the plea. However, the brain can only perform actions, or release domino chains, that exist to begin with. A normal individual would never have that homicidal domino chain at his disposal, and thus never run the threat of releasing it. That homicidal chain would have to have been created through experience[42], either as an involved witness, an involved accomplice, or through direct urging and teaching, and it would have to have been vivid and strong enough to be viable. The non-pathological homicidal person is directly responsible for his homicidal tendencies or domino chains. At some point in their

---

[42] All points and arguments in this book are exclusive of pathologies since they lie outside the book's philosophical context.

development these tendencies must have been engaged by the conscious mind, and once created can again be released consciously, or worse, reflexively.

Of course, the homicidal case illustrated by Goleman is an extreme one of neural hijacking, since we all have experienced neural hijackings at some point in our lives, points within which we cannot explain our behavior. Those points usually culminate in crying, shouting, even uncontrollable laughter, but rarely murder. Regardless, self-observation and self-awareness can provide a dampening effect to the point of reducing the chances of neural hijackings.

Another way in which self-awareness helps increase control over the impulsive will is by revealing to the observer both the causes and the effects of such impulses so that the observer can mitigate the former, and optimize the latter. For example, let us imagine a person who wishes to lose weight. That person can either be controlled by his hunger impulse by being blind and ignorant of it, or he can try to mollify it and direct it. By observing his hunger a person can learn when he is hungriest, what incites it the most, and toward what it is most intensely directed. By knowing when he is hungriest, a person can try to be busiest at those points to try to take his mind off his hunger (for example by being at work or at the gym); by learning what incites his hunger the most, he can try to reduce those activities (for example, watching TV or smoking marijuana); by learning toward what it is most intensely directed, the person can try to substitute similar things that are less caloric, such as substituting artificial sweeteners for sugars, salted celery for salt cravings, and tofu and Olestra for fat cravings. Only through observation and awareness can the person try to mitigate and redirect his will.

The last way in which self-awareness increases conscious control of the will is by evincing the lack of fulfillment or satisfaction of higher instinctual needs. Most, if not all, of the impulses can be traced back to the fulfillment of the basic instincts. If the higher-order fulfillment of those basic instincts is neglected, then the residual impulses become magnified in their effect and importance. For example, the less fulfilled we feel in life, and the more idle time we have, the more we feel the need to eat to feel internal satisfaction (not to say that eating is bad, but if performed out of boredom rather than need, it points to a higher-level problem). The nagging emptiness of unfulfillment invites satisfaction through more primal ways. Only through self-observation can we determine whether the satisfaction of those primal impulses is due to emptiness and boredom, or to the luxury of epicurean and romantic indulgence, or even to simple survival. Only through self-awareness will the answer be evinced.

Unpredictability of the Will

The will is basically reactive and embedded deeply within the human mind and body. We cannot control how we feel and how we impulsively are incited to react. The mental domino chains are automatically triggered by stimuli, also having already been formed through experience and instinct. In the example of the pioneering brothers and the bears, the sympathetic reflex is an automatic reflex, while the two distinct response options have been formed and cemented by experience and instinctual influence. The will induces the sympathetic response and then supplies the impulse to react in one of many ways. The conscious mind is thus incited into action and then given a range of options from which to choose.

Jealousy, desire, sympathy, and all the other impulses have been programmed into us through some mix of instinct and/ or experience. For instance, jealousy is a defense mechanism to threats to proprietary relationships. In order to incite us to action when a relationship with a spouse, child, or friend is under threat of replacement, human and/ or cultural evolution wound up with the feeling of jealousy. Without it, other people could court and steal a our mates without resistance, therefore compromising the chances of passing on our genes, or of maintaining relationships long enough to raise the offspring of those genes. Jealousy became an important tool for securing those relationships that increase our chances of procreation or successful upbringing of progeny.

Response patterns and human impulses, however, are like the weather in that they are essentially random and non-predictive since they are dependent on multiple, complex variables such as the environment and internal mental structures. We can predict weather patterns with very limited certainty because of the overwhelming number of variables involved, and because of the constantly changing conditions upon which the weather depends. As exaggerated by the renowned Butterfly Effect, the weather is so capricious that even seemingly insignificant events such as the flapping of wings by a butterfly can snowball and ultimately affect it. With so many possible things affecting the weather in such a constant and turbulent state of flux, predicting how it will change is impossible given that we cannot track the seemingly infinite number of variables. And even if we could track them all, by the mere fact of our tracking, we would influence them and thus change their behavior so that our measurement would be inaccurate. Similarly, we would never be able to predict someone's actions based on a set of initial conditions since the mind is continually receiving stimuli, some of them internally reflexive and some of them environmental, which affect the thought patterns and courses of action of a person. Although the simplistic parable of the pioneering brothers states two options, there are actually a multitude from which to choose since situations often resemble multiple prior experiences, each of which presents a different option to the individual. And since one situation is never exactly like a previous one, the difference between the new experience and the similar past one will provide the basis upon which to adapt the response.

Continuous stimulation also makes the mind highly adaptable since it is not locked into any one course of action but can

adapt its reactions as new situations surface. The mind starts
with a number of events, most of which are filtered out as insignificant. Those that pass through the filter trigger a number of
responses based on associations made through past experiences.
Those links may be purely analytical, such as association by physical characteristics like color or size, or they may be impulsive,
such as fear or desire. These new links in the chain are combined with the links from new, filtered events that trigger new
chains. The paths of the new chains are determined by the
strength of the link. For example, we've probably come across
multiple different cars in our past, but perhaps the sense of fear
that arises from an accident with one particular brand is so strong
that we always go down the path of triggering our survival instinct at the sight of that one kind. Or, perhaps with time that
link loses strength as we come across that brand of car day after
day, until finally other characteristics and other experiences drown
out our fear.

Like the weather, the mind is constantly being bombarded
by a seemingly infinite number of stimuli, each of which can mix
with the links of the current chain to lead to new chains. At any
one point in time the mind is actively pursuing a train of thought,
receiving visual, auditory, palpable, and olfactory information
based on the objects and situations surrounding the subject, receiving internal feed-forward and feedback information, as well
as digesting the internal physiological signals that the body produces. How the mind will mix, interpret, and in turn respond to
all the information is impossible to predict, even if the subject's
complete history is known. The mind, like the weather, is ultimately not very predictable.

The difference between the mind and the weather, however,
is that the former is actively filtering stimuli between those that
are worth noticing and those that are not. The weather reacts to
everything, while the mind actively filters inconsequential events
and focuses on those deemed most important to itself. In this
regard the mind reinforces its own behaviors and patterns, be-

coming slightly more predictable than otherwise. Obviously, the mind would tend to focus on those things with which it already has prior experience, increasing its experience with those things in question, selectively reinforcing its mental structures and its behavioral patterns. When witnessing a large number of cars passing us on a highway we would tend to focus on cars of the same makes and models as our own and ignore the rest, thereby reinforcing our knowledge of, and attitude toward, those cars. We would also look for features and qualities that would reinforce and validate those attitudes. If we liked the cars in question we would look for positive things, such as the attractiveness of the owners if the owners were attractive, or the attractiveness of the cars' condition.

In knowing which links within the network of chained events that comprise our past have had the most impact and are thus the strongest, we can anticipate our own reactions and thus influence or preempt them to suit us. We have to observe ourselves and study our pasts to gain insight into ourselves and others.

Breadth and Depth of Experience and the Will

In Chapter One we discussed how breadth and depth are factors in the attribution of value. In terms of the mental domino chains, the greater the depth and breadth of experiences we go through, the larger the number of links and options from which to react. Since we are bound to react to stimuli, internal or external, and those reactions are partially based on the recording of events of past experiences, then the more experiences and past events, the more links emanating from the dominos of the chain, and the more adaptive the response to the stimulus can be.

To take an extreme as an example, let us imagine a jungle tribesman who has never seen a car. If confronted by one while alone, he would have no idea what to make of it or do with it. He has had no experience with cars, and therefore would not know how to react to the sight of one, but probably would inspect it curiously. On the other hand, a typical American adult sees cars on a daily basis and has no problem identifying and using one. Although faced with the exact situation, two different people react in completely different ways based on their past experiences, and predictably so. Each had a number of options from which to choose in reacting to the situation, but because the American had experience with cars, he had a larger range of options in this particular scenario, and therefore a greater chance of reacting optimally to the situation at hand.

We are completely bounded by our experiences, and therefore defined by them and our innate instincts. Like a car that can only travel down roads that have been previously paved, we can only react in ways defined by our experiences. To expect the tribesman to get into the car, turn the ignition key, and drive away would be ludicrous. Our responses to the situations we encounter in our daily lives are bounded by our experiences with past ones. The more we have encountered situations similar to the one being confronted at a point in time, the larger the range of response options from which to choose, the larger the chance that the response chosen was the most suitable or beneficiary.

If we wanted to get from point A to point B and had never traveled between the two points, then we would probably not be able to choose the fastest or cheapest way to get there since we would not know which traveling option was fastest or cheapest. The only way to know, besides asking other people who know, would be to travel between the two points through various paths, multiple times. The more paths and the more times we traveled between points A and B, the likelier we would be to finding the fastest or cheapest way. New Yorkers, for example, are famous for having favorite "quick" routes to the different landmarks in and out of the city.

Obviously, past experiences need not necessarily be direct, they could also be vicarious through communication with others. But regardless of the means, this type of reasoning would suggest that the more adept a person desires to be regarding a certain situation or phenomenon, the larger the number of experiences, vicarious or direct, that that person needs to have regarding the situation or phenomenon.

William James takes it a bit further and states that not only are we bounded by the range of our experiences, our past experiences actually blind us to other possibilities through habit formation and the comfort of the known:

> "Each of these [choices made in life] carries with it an insensibility to *other* opportunities and occasions-an insensibility which can only be described physiologically as an inhibition of new impulses by the habit of old ones already formed. . . . a habit, once grafted on an instinctive tendency, restricts the range of the tendency itself, and keeps us from reacting on any but the habitual object, although other objects might just as well have been chosen had they been the first-comers."

However obvious James' line of reasoning might seam, its implications are not. Human beings have a finite number of experiences in their lives, a limited number of years to live. Thus, they cannot experience everything they wish or imagine to experience. Being effective warrants focusing one's experiences to limited types of situations. Experiencing life without focusing those experiences will produce individual choices to many stimuli, but will not produce multiple choices to specific stimuli. Instead of having few domino chains, each with many branches, you will have many domino chains with few branches. You will be able to respond to many different situations, but the response will be suboptimal to those many situations. Compare this to guessing how to respond to many situations, most of which will never be encountered, but at the same time knowing how to respond optimally to a specific few. It's the jack-of-all-trades, master-of-none argument.

Building an expertise warrants depth of experience versus breadth. It implies experiencing a situation in many different ways, versus experiencing many different types of situations once. However, the key in achieving depth is to differ the experience, not to repeat it. Doing the same thing the same way time after time does not add branches of domino chains. Only changing variables and responses to situations will create depth. Thus, change is imperative, even small change, versus habit and routine. Change must be actively sought, or our 'insensibility to other opportunities' will take hold.

Achieving Focus

The adaptation of our instincts into personal traits or reaction mechanisms is a crude response to our past experiences and not fully suitable to every future situation we encounter. For instance, let us say a person was a survivor of a plane crash, and developed a fear of flying because of it. At face value it is a suitable response from our survival instinct, but in application, it is absurd since flying is one of the safest forms of transportation. Driving somewhere rather than flying would not be rational since statistically it would be more dangerous. But our innate survival instinct would build in this fear as an adaptive response to the trauma of the accident. Understanding where the fear comes from and what drives it would enable us to make a rational decision regarding its application. Only when we understand the underlying instincts and drives that motivate us can we strive toward reaching fulfillment through the satisfaction of higher-level needs, rather than the constant yet temporal satisfaction of base impulses. Once we have achieved a focus based on realizing our highest level of worth, the other fragments of life that fall outside of focus lose their appeal and importance.

The importance of focus is exemplified by the story of the child who is riding his bicycle down the street. He notices a rock in his path, so he focuses on it until he unwittingly runs into it and falls. His problem was that he fixated on the rock, rather than the path around it, so that he wound up riding right into it. Similarly, as long as we do not have foci in life, our minds will pay attention to the smaller, more temporal and base needs that arise, rather than focusing on those things that would yield longer-term fulfillment. As long as our minds and attention are idle, we have the time and capacity to be distracted by every pittance that arises. But if our minds are focused on the things we have determined are most important, being idle and distracted becomes difficult. That is not to say we should be stubborn and stick to whatever we deem important solely based on the information we had some time past, and discount everything else. In fact, the opposite should be the case. We should be constantly reevaluating our philosophies since values do shift as we mature. But as a result of having focus, our capacity for idleness decreases substantially, ensuring that our actions lead to a more rewarding and fulfilling life.

Part Three:

External Currents

Chapter 7.

Reality, Relativity, and Relevance

Relying on Absolutes

As human beings, we are fallible in every way. We are fallible in how we sense what we experience, in how we respond to it, in how we learn from it, and in how we store and recall it. Our senses are fallible, and thus might not detect and interpret sense data correctly, misleading us. Hallucinations, illusions, and ear ringing are all testaments to the fallibility of our different senses. Miscommunications and differing accounts of events between witnesses are testaments to the fallibility of our mind and its processes. Human memory is reconstructive in nature, and not a type of machine that can record and play back events like video cameras[43]. When we memorize a face or a setting we do not take a mental picture and store it, instead we separately memorize different physical profiles, different physical and abstract attributes such as colors, temperatures, and emotions, and then associate all the memories into a recalled perception according to a characteristic that ties them together, such as time, place, or name.

---

[43] Damasio pgs. 100-105

When I remember looking at my friend yesterday, for example, I put together the pieces of that event to come up with a total memory. I separately store the two-dimensional outlines of her figure, the colors of her clothes, the smell of her perfume, the emotion I felt at the moment, and the sounds I heard, including her voice. I take all those separate pieces of information and put them together according to that which ties them, her name and the date or time, to form a complete memory of the event. As my memory of that moment fades I start to forget parts such as colors and sounds, and may even unconsciously piece other memories into the event to fill gaps. I thus start forming a fuzzy or altered memory of the event as its importance and relevance fades.

Our perceived memories are highly fallible since any or all of the individual memorized profiles or attributes, or the links holding our memories together, could blur, change, or fail at any point in time.

Although we are fallible in every way, Western man still has been plagued by the illusion of an absolute reality, or an absolute truth, to take comfort in its simplicity and finality. As we gain more experience and confidence with our senses we tend to forget that they are both merely interpretive and wholly fallible, creating the false belief that what we perceive is true, that the reality that unfolds before is indisputable. This is the direct result of physical necessity—as we interact with our environment we must often be swift and unwavering, necessitating complete confidence in our perceptions. For example, as we drive a car, we must often react within seconds or milliseconds of occurrences in order to avoid accidents and maneuver adroitly, requiring an unconscious steely confidence in our senses and our perceptions. For us to at all question or doubt what we perceive during the heat of the moment would preclude us from reacting properly, making us inept drivers. Metaphysically, as our experiences compound and reinforce our confidence in our senses and perceptions, our conscious mind translates this confidence as meaning that an absolute reality exists, and our senses are infallible in their perception; although perhaps it is us that are sometimes fallible in our interpretation of them. How is it otherwise that day-in and day-out we can interact with the world so skillfully? Plato compounded the problem by introducing the notion of his Platonic Forms or absolute ideals, or that everything perceived is but a less-than-perfect image of an absolute object—an absolute form which cannot be perceived but can be understood. Although he did acknowledge that perception is flawed, he still clung to the notion of absolutes, except this time the absolutes came to exist in the understanding rather than in perception. This notion of Platonic Forms, still with is today millennia after Plato, is solidly entrenched in Western man's mind. The religions that sprung up before, during, and after Plato caused this entrenchment since they often reinforced his notions of Forms with the notions of perfect deities and absolute codes of morals and truths. Thus not only does the physical world reflect absolute form, human behavior reflects absolute codes of conduct.

Believing that what we see, read, hear, or remember is all absolutely true and real is easy and comforting because we can act and behave without second thoughts. However, despite the comfort of absolutes, and as a direct result of our fallibility and the subjective nature of existence, absolute reality does not exist. The lack of exactitude has been argued again and again by countless philosophers, starting with the positivistic philosophy of Auguste Comte, the French philosopher considered the father of sociology and positivism, and continuing then on.

Instead of realities, what we encounter are perceptions and our interpretations of our surroundings. Sight, smell, touch, and the other senses all contribute to these overall perceptions, but even together they do not constitute a true reality. For instance, we cannot see infrared light. Does that mean that it is not real, or that it does not exist? Of course not. It means that it is not part of our visual perception. Similarly, if we are hallucinating and see pink butterflies flapping their wings around us, does that mean that they are "real"? No, it means we perceive them, and we probably need a good rest, but it does not necessarily mean that they are real. They are real in the sense that they exist in our minds, but they do not physically affect us. Does light travel in a straight line as we assume? Not if measured over great distances since Einstein showed that gravity affects its path in the space-time continuum. To further remove us from our comfortable notion of absolute reality, Einstein's theories of relativity also showed that time and space are not constant but flexible to gravity and motion. Two people can theoretically witness the same event but perceive a different sequence, both observations being correct according to the relative motion of the two people. Neither is wrong in their observation of the event; the problem is that the "reality"[44] of an event is subject-dependent, or relative.

But a true reality still seems to exist, regardless of how we perceive it. Well, how could we ever come to know this reality if we will forever be bounded by our perceptions? Our inability to verify anything puts us in a situation similar to Schroedinger's situation with his hypothetical cat[45].

Schroedinger was a physicist who wrote a letter to Einstein trying to explain his view of the paradox that arises when trying to define the existence of something at a point in time without direct and empirical knowledge of that something. He used the following analogy to illustrate his view. Imagine a box containing a live cat, a vial of poison, and a machine that will break the vial open once a certain atom has decayed (interpret this as meaning that the vial could break at any random moment in time). The cat could die at any moment, but we cannot know

---

[44] From here on I will leave out the quotations around "reality," assuming the reader understands that in this book the notion of reality is understood to be a subject-dependent phenomenon devoid of absolutes, and thus different from the notion used colloquially.

[45] The original paradox was written by Schroedinger as an illustration of the paradox of the dual nature of electrons as both particles and waves. However, the philosophical crossover is noted here. As was noted before, and as seen here, philosophy and the sciences have significantly influenced each other throughout history.

whether he is dead or alive at any given point in time unless we peek inside the box. Schroedinger stipulated that as long as we do not check, the cat is neither dead nor alive, yet he is also both dead and alive. His exact status is an indefinable paradox.

One of the resultant observations of the cat paradox is that reality is an observer-dependent phenomenon. In other words, reality only exists as long as someone is there to define the concept, and then conceive and observe it. Like many other words, reality is defined by humans and completely subject to their existence and conception. The notion had no meaning before humans invented it. To wonder what reality was like during the age of the dinosaur is to wonder whether purple monsters have green eyes or blue ones. It makes no sense because both are human creations.

We will never know if the cat with the corked poison in the box is dead until we check inside the box, and we will never know whether the veracity or precision of a perceived reality is as it seems without extrinsic verification. A cardboard wall separates Schroedinger and his cat in the paradox, while the wall between our mind and a physical phenomenon is our senses. The caveat with reality is that we cannot check, peek, nor verify. In other words, any conceivable method of ascertaining the reality of an occurrence will make use of one or more of our senses. Our only contact with the external world is our senses, and therefore any way of checking reality will have to involve our senses, *which we have already determined are fallible and not dependable.*

To throw another wrench into the machine, according to Heisenberg's Uncertainty Principle[46], another theory from physics relevant to the relativity of life, we cannot describe objects except as characteristic measurements, but then we are limited

---

[46] Werner Heisenberg, a quantum physicist, stated in his Uncertainty Principle that it is possible to either know the position of an electron with great accuracy to the detriment of knowing its momentum, or vice-versa. Measuring one affects the other with uncertain effects. This is true of anything at any scale, although at larger scales the uncertainty becomes relatively irrelevant.

in the degrees of freedom in which we are allowed to measure something. In other words, we only know of things through observation and measurement, but then we distort that something the minute we try to measure or observe it. Not only are our senses fallible because they are distortable, they also distort everything with which they come into contact, changing that which they "sense." But we are stuck, depending on them in full. The world around us is uncertain merely by the fact that we exist in it. Although for most practical purposes we can ignore the miniscule changes we impose upon something we measure or observe, the principle nonetheless has important ramifications for philosophy. We are always participants in one way or another of the events that we witness, and as such always influence those events, making us biased observers.

We will never know if an absolute reality exists because we all will forever be bound by personal interpretation. Even if one million people say that a car is blue, it only takes one to say it's black to make things inconclusive. We will label him color blind and conclude it's blue, but numbers alone do not make an absolute reality. He sees it differently, and for him it will always be black. Period. He will live his life with a black car, and the rest of us will live with a blue one. But we will never truly "know" the color of that car. And it will never really matter either, because we will act based on our perceptions of the car, and those actions and their results will be in accordance with our personal perceptions.

As Immanuel Kant, the eighteenth-century German philosopher theorized, it is our apprehension of the world and not the world itself that determines behavior. The world we perceive and to which we react is the world for which we were created to perceive. In other words, we perceive the world according to how our mind is structured to think, and according to how our senses were built to sense. The world perceived by a dog is a completely different from that which we perceive. To them it is a mostly a world of smells, to us it is mostly a world of colored sights. Our knowledge of the world is *a priori* ordained according to how our minds are structured to conceive of space, time, and what Kant called the Categories of understanding, things such as substance and causality. A cat is not necessarily an animal with four legs, whiskers, slits for eyes, and so on. According to a dog, a cat is a thing that smells this or that way, or to a mosquito a cat is a thing that tastes this or that way. What defines a cat is determined by the structures of knowledge and perception, our understanding as the cat is perceived in the spatiotemporal and categorical world our minds create. And how we perceive a cat will rule how we react to it. If a cat is nice to look at or nice to the touch, we will want to pet him, if a cat smells "bad," a dog will want to scare it away, if it tastes "good," a mosquito will want suck its blood.

To Kant, how and in what way we know things is determined by how and in what way we perceive of space, time, and the Categories of knowledge. For example, we know space to be three dimensional, we know time to move forward in imperceptible steps, and we understand causation through association. These three mental components together comprise our understanding. But from our discussions herein regarding the extensive influence of the instincts on knowledge and behavior, a fourth basic component to the understanding seems to fit. And that is intent. How and what we know about things is largely determined by our instinctual intent towards those things. A thing is known to us both according to its physical characteristics as perceived by our senses and its abstract characteristics as perceived by our emotions. In both cases, the instincts play a large role in determining how the information is received and stored to form an encompassing perception of an object or phenomenon. All memories have embedded instinctual intent, and all behavior is seeded by the same. Knowledge, understanding, and reason all are inextricably intertwined in the mind with their impetus and reason for being, instinctual intent. We know of things, understand things, and do things because those things possess meaning vis-à-vis my instincts, and that meaning comes to life through intent. Back to the example of the abstract definition of a cat, it is also a thing that is "good" because it brings comfort, or it is "bad" because it induces sneezing, or has some other associated abstract emotion, depending on cats' meaning to the instincts and the instincts' ensuing intent toward cats. We know the world and interact with it according to its meaning to our instincts, and the intent implied by it. To say we understand the world only according to our spatiotemporal and categorical structures, but leave out instinctual intent, is to assume a robotic, passive, and objective mind. We are never objective, never passive, and always human, which means that we exist to know the world as it relates to us and our instincts, and never in any other way.

With such an uncertain and phenomenological existence, Kant claimed that science, embedded in that world of pure apprehension, is thus a categorical description of the human experience, and not necessarily a set of immutable laws in want of discovery. Science is not found, like a new continent, but created, like a new electrical appliance. Science is another language and tool of human evolution, used to communicate and progress. In fact, quantum physics has reached the point where its incomprehensibility to human understanding has started to blur its distinction from philosophy. Theories are now lauded because of their level of fit, rather than their experimental viability and repeatability. And now that we've added intent as a basic epistemological component, Kant's view of science takes on a new relevance, with science also being a tool of that intent.

A Matter of Perception

Relativity and relativism are rather brutal paradigms for the mind to wrestle. Absolutes are very comforting. Black is black, white is white, wrong is wrong and right is right. But are they? If we can't trust ourselves to know even the most basic principles, how can we trust ourselves to know anything as true?

Well, we can't. We just simply have to come to terms with the fact that we will always live in a world built upon the shaky ground of personal perception, where nothing is necessarily as it seems. An extension, and example, of this is the illusion of the separation between perceived phenomena and objects in time and space, when instead the world we perceive is a completely internal construct. It is akin to watching a movie and becoming so involved that we begin to believe we are personally immersed in the story, when we know that it is merely entertainment on a flat screen. The world we engage is completely made up of our ideas and perceptions, even though we seem to be intractably immersed in a physical environment.

Black could be blue, blue could be black, and we will never know anything for sure. But this should not be, and in general is not, paralyzing. Every time we make a decision, we make that decision holding implicit assumptions about the factors involved in reaching our conclusions. Every time we talk to someone on the phone, we assume that we are talking to the person whose voice matches that voice we hold in memory. Someone else could be faking that voice, or have a similar voice, or be generating a digitized replica, or our memory might have gotten mixed up. But in order to make the phone worth its use, we have to make a large number of assumptions every time we pick up the receiver.

The verification of an absolute reality is impossible, and we act based on reasonable assumptions. We live in the world our minds create, and everything that occurs must go through the same filters and apply to the same personal frames of reference. So it doesn't matter if I say you are moving at ten mph, or whether you say that it is I who is moving at ten mph, since we both will act as if we alone stood still, and everything in our world will behave according to that interpretation, and it will make sense. But what if a bystander entered the picture and also said that I was the one in motion, or if according to our perception a building also seemed to be moving at ten mph? Then I would be more likely to alter my perception and believe that in fact I was the one in motion.

Because we know we are fallible and bound by our senses, we ground ourselves to the opinions of the majority and the majority of the physical evidence. The majority view is most likely to be the most apposite view against which we should react and adapt. Of course, that's entirely qualitative, and some people's opinions and some sorts of evidence hold more weight than others. For example, we weigh our friends' opinions in higher regard than a stranger's, all other things being equal. Similarly, and barring physical impairments, we tend to hold optical evidence in higher regard than auditory evidence. But in general, whenever opinions diverge or evidence is contradicted, we tend to go with the majority view.

As was alluded to in the "Validation and Adaptation" section, we have actually made a science out of figuring out what conclusion is more reasonable. That science is probability theory and statistics. Probability theory will tell you what's more probable based on weighing the numbers. But probability theory and statistics will never give you a definite conclusion, which is an important point to consider. Even when something is probable one time in a million, it is still probable and cannot be discounted, although rationally we would (well, most of the time—let us not forget the popularity of state lotteries). For example, in Columbus' time it seemed highly improbable that the earth was round. But as far as we know today, based on new evidence, that seems to be the most probable case. Probabilities can and do change, so that nothing can be discounted, and nothing can be taken as absolutely true. But in general, the more opinions and physical evidence we can get to confirm something, the more that something is probable, and the more we take it as a reasonable assumption.

But if there is no right or wrong, true or false, then how can we define "probability"? "Probably" seems to imply comparison against an absolute. However, the answer lies not in absolute truth but in consistent truth. In other words, when something is probable, that does not mean that there is a high certainty that it did or will happen. Rather, it means that something agrees with past and future perceptions and experiences with high certainty.

For example, consider a forecast of ninety percent rain tomorrow. It should be read as saying that with ninety percent probability what will happen tomorrow will agree with the forecaster's notion of rain. We may experience sprinkling tomorrow, in which case he might say he was right, but I'll disagree because to me a sprinkle is not rain. Or what if a city experienced rain only on the west side? The people on the east side did not experience rain and would not agree with the forecast, yet the people on the west side would, even though they may all have been in the same city. In either case, can we say that it absolutely rained?

Nothing can be proven without a doubt, but we can rationally assume that something exists using probability. Of course, this is all done within the context of our own perspective of the world, since that's the only connection we have with our surroundings.

Most of us as children have been mesmerized by the fact that if we hold something close to our faces, that something will seem to change position depending on which eye is open. If our left eyes are open, then objects seem to be located to the right. If we then close our left eyes and open our right ones, objects "jump" to the left. We know that the objects have not moved in relation to us, but our eyes seem to deceive us and say that they have. So where are the objects? To the right or to the left? Well, that depends on which eyes are open. The answer is unimportant. We act according to what eyes we have open. If objects are to the left, than everything else will adjust in our sights so that what we perceive make sense. When we try to reach for objects, our hands' positions will also be determined by the same eyes with which we see the objects, so that they will also be to the left of us when they get close, and we will be able to grab the objects without missing them. If we open our other eyes, then both the objects and our hands will jump positions, and again we will be able to grab the objects without missing them. They are different perceptions, but neither are right nor wrong. Regardless, everything is in the right relative place, allowing us to act and behave with our surroundings.

Well, if we don't know whether the car is black or blue, or whether our house is beige or white, or whether we are creations of an extraterrestrial being or a chance occurrence in time, how do we know that anything with which we interact exists, or for that matter, how do we know we exist? The existence of other things is unimportant for the same reason that describing the finger as being to the left or right is unimportant. That we perceive them is enough.

A Relevant Existence

We have determined that absolute reality is impossible to validate and that the existence of anything is without proof, including our existence as human beings. Questioning our own existence puts everything into a tailspin. Any proof we conjure up will be tainted by our perceptions. Why then should we seek a fulfillment that is mired in our perception of the world, or why is fulfillment even important to begin with?

What we can say in fact is that we have perceptions, we have thoughts. Descarte's "I think therefore I am" rings true. Although we cannot prove anything about ourselves or our surroundings conclusively, we do know we exist in the form of our thoughts because of the mere fact that we can even doubt our existence. Our thoughts exist; we can say this because they lie *inside* our sensual or perceptual wall.

Given that we exist solely within the context of our own interpretations of our surroundings, it doesn't matter whether the surroundings in general are illusory or real, anything lying within our realm—and that's everything—can be questioned or doubted. With that in mind, how do we deal with solipsism? How do we know that we, as human beings and not just as a series of thoughts, exist? We cannot prove it in absolute, and we cannot prove it with certainty within our world of reference.

As was argued by the Pragmatic philosophers, the problem of solipsism really is irrelevant. Whether we exist in this form or another, or whether something is true or real in absolute terms, are unimportant as long as the reality we perceive is consistent and sane to us. As long as the events in our memories are consistent with the events we sense, and those same events unfold within reason according to our expectations, then we can retain sanity and interact with the world we sense, thereby being granted the ability of obtaining satisfaction through those interactions. In other words, a reality, or rather life, is significant when we have the ability to interact within it to the reasonable satisfaction of our desires and needs. Reason states that we should not expect Nirvana since emotional highs necessitate the lows for existence, and conversely we should not expect a hell on earth, either. However, if we can control our own bodies and influence the environments about us in ways that make us happy in general, then the realities we perceive are as real as they need to be.

There is no set of criteria by which we can judge the level of reality of a perception, therefore our yardstick should measure the fitness of a perception to our expectations of what life should yield. If a perceived reality measures up, then so be it. If it does not, then we should search for whatever might be wrong.

The question no longer is, "Am I really a human being receiving sense data that is consistent with an absolute reality?" since the term "absolute" no longer makes sense. Instead we should be asking ourselves, "Am I satisfied with the world as I perceive it, and can I interact with it to obtain those things that fulfill and make me happy?"

Only when our interactions with the worlds we perceive become dysfunctional in any way should we start worrying about discordance between the realities perceived and the realities that we believe we should be perceiving. If we no longer can obtain reasonable satisfaction from our interactions with the worlds perceived, then we have to start questioning the proper function of our senses, neurological conditions, or even senses of reality. Perhaps our eyesight have deteriorated and can no longer see well enough to be self supportive, in which case we need glasses. Perhaps we have developed manic-depression and our extreme mood swings are hampering our abilities to interact with our surroundings, in which case perhaps lithium or other drugs might help. Or perhaps we believe in a grander justice pervading the world, but now things no longer seem to balance out, which causes us much stress and worry. Perhaps in this case we may have to switch beliefs to the idea that justice is a human invention without application outside of human constructs.

Regardless of how we perceive things, the causes and the effects of all phenomena are observed through the same senses, sustaining causal relationships and making reality flow. As long as the way in which we perceive the world remains constant, the notion of ulterior realities is irrelevant. What would be of concern is if we couldn't trust our senses to observe and interpret things in a constant fashion. Then reality would not flow, and we would not be able to interpret causal relationships and act on our perceptions of things.

Perhaps the world we perceive is being spoon-fed to us by an alien being through some sort of deception, perhaps through a machine neurally connected to our central nervous system. But as long as our perceptions measure up on the yardsticks we create, the notion of deception is trivial. The only things that matter are those that we have the power to influence or by which we are influenced.

Freedom of Self-invention

In order to be free to search for fulfillment we must be will-
ing to give up our attachments to the world that we perceive. We
must realize our independence from everything outside ourselves,
and thus must let go of not only the notions of absolute truths
and realities to which we chain ourselves, but also to any other
external phenomena from which we yield a personal definition.

To William James, the self is made up of all those things a
person calls his own, including his mind, his body, his relationships, and his physical possessions. The idea of ownership implies the singular "me." When something is "mine," it belongs to
me, and thus is necessarily a part of me through that relationship
of possession. As the ego identifies with something, it incorpo-
rates it into its own vision of itself. From thus stems jealousy,
greed, and protectiveness. An affront to anything related to the
individual is an affront to himself, and the more he possesses the
larger the individual's vision of his self.

As we, however, own more, and as we grow to attribute more
and more external objects and relationships to ourselves, the
more vulnerable we become. With more possessions and deeper
attributions between the self and its possessions, the more ways
the ego can become threatened. Instead of concentrating on
important matters, the ego can become occupied by constantly
fighting brush fires.

To the Buddhist monk, the answer is to disavow possessions
and break the connection between the ego and its external ties.
The soul then becomes free to act irrespective of all things mundane. Without possessions, the self can live without fear of af-
fronts to itself through worldly means. The monks have no objects of value to be broken, no relationships to be stolen, no
vanity of body to be ridiculed. This philosophy falls exactly in
line with the traditionalist definition of freedom, whereby one
seeks to eliminate obstacles.

To existentialists, however, obstacles are an essential com-

ponent of freedom, just as possessions are a necessary component of the self. Without stimulus, without objects at which to
aim mental intention, consciousness threatens to collapse into
nothingness. Freedom lies in the distance between the objects of
consciousness, which provide both the stimuli and the targets of
mental intention, and the phenomenon of consciousness. This
distance, which exists as nothing (i.e. is in the mind and is not
physically real), is the basis of freedom. The notions in my mind,
my perception of objects, the ideas that circulate, are all intangible creations according to the states of my brain through the
passage of time. But taken in an instance in time, those mental
phenomena do not exist, and thus consciousness does not exist.
It cannot be seen, felt, heard, or graphed. Its whole existence
vanishes into nothingness. But consciousness too is an important component of the self.

We beget consciousness, and thus an existence antithetical
to nothingness, through the exercise of freedom in making
choices and aiming mental intent. Consciousness is not a physical object like a book or a table, it is not an organ like the brain,
and neither is it the sum of electrical signals travelling through
the brain. Consciousness is an abstract concept representing
dynamic mental positions and states. It is unattached to the physical world except through the physiological phenomenon of sensation. The conscious mind receives sense data and forms perceptions of the physical world through that data. But the conscious mind itself, not being part of the physical world, cannot
interact with that world except through the manifestation of its
intentions through the body. Though we cannot see other people's
conscious minds, and they cannot see ours, we can profile their
minds through the physical manifestations of their actions. Although someone's actions do not holistically define someone's
mind, they present a profile of it and its physical intentions.

Consciousness comes into existence similar to how the wind
comes into existence. The wind is not a tangible object you can
grab or see, that you can put in a box for later enjoyment. Like

consciousness, it is dependent on time. If we stopped the motion of time in one particular instance, the wind would vanish, and all we would be left with is its body—air. It has a tenuous existence and "knows" of things as it encounters them; flowing around buildings and gaining speed as a consequence; feeling the contours of mountains and hills and getting direction in the process; interacting with birds and planes so they can gain lift and fly. But the wind is not the hills and buildings that give it shape and speed. It is a force that is molded by them, that is given existence by the presence of all those objects and the air that surrounds those objects—but it is not them. It goes through them and around them, but always continues on independent of them. Wind's freedom lies within this flirtation of independence that threatens it into destruction. Although the wind is independent of the buildings and contours of the earth it encounters, it can only exist while they do, while they give it speed and direction. Without those contours, the wind would cease to exist.

The wind is nothing, given an evanescent existence by the objects around it. It is free because it is nothing to begin with, nothing to end with, and independent of all things in between. Thus is consciousness. It is nothing to begin with, nothing to end with, and independent of all things in between. The wind is not the air that encases it, and consciousness is not the body that contains it. The wind is not the objects it flows through, and consciousness is not the objects it senses—it is not the names it is given nor the past that follows it. Like the wind, it is free because it is nothing to begin with, to end with, and at all instances in between, and it is free because it is independent of all things.

Just like our actions constitute a profile of our minds, our physical attributes, historical past, possessions, and our exhibited thoughts also pluralistically profile our selves. For example, we can create artistic sketches of people by looking at them, but those sketches are not them, and we are not touching them or looking at them when we touch and look at that sketches. Similarly, we can sketch people's selves by witnessing their behaviors, noting their physical characteristics and possessions, and creating biographies of their pasts, but all those profiles together do not constitute their selves in-and-of-themselves. People's selves are physically untouchable and unknowable. We could only *know* people by being them.

In essence, the mind and the self are abstractly separated, where the self is the dualistic sum of someone's profiling characteristics *and* his inscrutable mind. Sartre asserts that freedom is exactly that separation between mind, profiling characteristics, and person. Since I, "I" being my mind, am not necessarily my person, I have the freedom to act independently of it. I do not have to be my history, I can act in spite of it[47]. I can be brave despite typically behaving cowardly. I can be forward, despite historically behaving timidly. I am not timid because I typically behave that way, I am whatever I choose to be. Similarly, I am not short, fat, green, nor muscular, for example, because my body is that way. I am a changing self constantly being redefined. But the physical attributes of the body to which I am attached are short, fat, green, and muscular. I need not behave like a bully because my body is muscular, and I need not have a Napoleonic complex because my body is short. Because the self is to some degree independent of the body, I can behave in whichever way I choose, regardless of my person. Freedom lies in the individual's ability to transcend his physical persona, his historical behavior, his possessions, his family, and all other things that are commonly referred in the first person.

Having an attachment to possessions is not binding if I appreciate the fact that the attachment is illusory. I need to be able

---

[47] Some people might note that this seems to be in conflict with the idea that the "I" can only act as his experience allows him, being bounded by the choices, or domino chains, presented through experience. Although this still holds true, freedom exists where the mind chooses among the options experience presents it, despite the historical way in which the person has acted. Just because historically I've been assertive, I do not necessarily need to define myself as an assertive person. I know how to act insouciantly, and have the freedom to do so despite my historical behavior.

to let go of the attachment when necessary, and thus maintain a psychological distance. Similarly, metaphysically speaking, I am not my historical self in that by thinking of my past self I am objectifying it, and thus thinking "not me." My past self is an object to my self like a rock is an object, something to be thought of in the third person, something from which I can act independently. Although I feel emotions in regards to the past and have ties born of repercussions and consequences, those emotions and ties are all mental constructs[48]. I can act and behave now regardless of what I did yesterday because the me of yesterday is not the me of now. If I made plans and promises yesterday for today, I can behave today despite those plans and promises because nothing tethers or bounds me metaphysically to those plans and promises (but it might get people to question my sense of honor!). I am not the rock in the ground because I can act and behave despite the rock.

Let us use a car as an example. A car is the sum of all its parts—engine, headlights, chairs—plus its potential for motion. A car is not just its physical characteristics, its engine for example, nor is it just its persona, or in this case its potential for motion. A car that has a big engine and the body of an SUV is not necessarily an off-road vehicle, and it does not have to be driven off-road only. And a car that has only been driven in racing tracks, having a racing history, is not necessarily a "race car."

And lastly, but most importantly, I am also not necessarily my mind nor its functions. We saw in Chapter Five that the brain can act without its own knowledge (as in the commissurotomy experiment); and that it is fault-tolerant—meaning that I could have an accident and lose the ability to speak English, yet still function in all other ways. After those events I would still be the metaphysical "me," yet physically different in a significant way.

The human dilemma then becomes one of self-invention. It

---

[48] I am not denying the importance of the past to the self and its interaction with the world. Promises, consequences, and expectations are all imperatives of a functioning modern society. But history is only a part of the self, not its entirety, and this has consequences for the self and its freedom through independence.

is not for us to ponder who or what we are, but instead to ponder who are what we want to be. Our physical characteristics are malleable, our histories are written by the decisions we ourselves make, our minds are a loose connection of dispensable functions (to the sense of self), and our behavior is embedded in the freedoms of choice. To say that we need to "find" ourselves during our teenage years or during our midlife crisis implies that there is an immutable something to be found. In reality what we need to do is create ourselves, continuously. If we have reached a midlife crisis it is because we have become inauthentic and forsaken our freedoms. Our identity crises are instead continual opportunities of being.

But, Sartre contends, the freedoms of being are extremely difficult to bear. The burden of responsibility and accountability of choice, and the appalling abyss of nothingness, frightens us away. To acknowledge that we have this freedom is to look at nothingness straight in the face, to know that we are a transient wind, that otherwise we are nothing. In other words, to understand and believe that we are not just our physical characteristics, our histories, our habits, and our actions, but to instead believe that we are the continuous creation of all those things *and* our fleeting thoughts, our independent consciousness, is to understand that at every instant we are standing on the edge of annihilation into Nothingness. Get rid of our physical characteristics, or more importantly and more easily, get rid of our minds, and you get rid of us.

As comforting as thinking that a dead body holds a piece of the person that inhabited it in times past can be, it does not. And as comforting as thinking that a person lives on in the memories of others can be, he does not. Aborting our freedoms and believing that we are our physical characteristics and our pasts is far more comfortable, and thus deny nothingness its essence. It is comforting to believe that even without our thoughts, we are still the something physical and historical left behind. But we are also the choices we face in the face of experience and environment. Remove stimuli and physical phenomena, or remove the passage of time, and our consciousness collapses and ceases to exist. Our consciousness becomes nothingness, and thus we ourselves become nothingness, because what is left, just our physical attributes and our history, is not us.

Inertia also blinds us. It is far easier to follow the same behavioral patterns, the same routines, and make the same choices, as we have always done. When we come to believe that we are something or someone specifically, when others come to have expectations about us, when they come to believe that we are the sum of the things we have done and the choices we have made, yanking ourselves from those perceptions at every moment in time to act freely and independently is very difficult. The inertia of our actions carries us with little added risk or work on our part, and to let it do so is comforting. Meeting expectations, whatever those expectations may be, mitigates any repercussions. The new and unexpected carry the most risk because they impart the most responsibility.

Denying ourselves freedom from extrinsic definition, however, is also a choice. Believing that our essence is physical and historical is not "wrong," but we must understand that in believing this we are denying ourselves a certain freedom. We are now ruled by our past, by our physical attributes, and by expectations. We save ourselves the burden of freedom, and we save ourselves from having to stare at the abyss of nothingness, but we also compromise our abstract self with our physical and historical persona. We are no longer a master of our circumstances, taking things as they come and for what they are worth to us, responding selectively. Instead we become an arrow in time, thrusting forward incessantly regardless of the winds about us. To not become this arrow in time and truly project the self into the future and seek perfection, man needs to maintain a separation with his self.

By detaching the mind from the body in forming the concept of the self, we become free to live purely by abstract rules such as principles, or by no rules at all. We can freely reinvent ourselves at every step, and can live life in ways otherwise impossible, reach goals otherwise unreachable. We can make any choice, or no choice at all, and bear full responsibility, good and bad. But whatever repercussions our actions yield, whatever paths and turns we take, we'll never have any regrets because we know we chose them freely. We'll look back on life and know it was the best attainable life because it was the one we chose, rather than the one we followed.

Chapter 8.

The Imperative of Choice

Likewise and during every day of an illustrious life, time carries us. But a moment always comes when we have to carry it. We live in the future: "tomorrow," "later on," "when you have made your way," "you will understand when you're old enough." Such irrelevancies are wonderful, for, after all, it's a matter of dying. Yet a day comes when a man notices or says that he is thirty. Thus he asserts his youth. But simultaneously he situates himself in relation to time. He takes his place in it. He admits that he stands at a certain point on a curve that he acknowledges having to travel to its end. He belongs to time, and by the horror that seizes him, he recognizes his worst enemy. Tomorrow, he was longing for tomorrow, whereas everything in him ought to reject it. That revolt of the flesh is the absurd.

Albert Camus

An Absurd Existence

There is an absurdity in existence, an absurdity that is realized in those moments when there is a "divorce between man
and his life, the actor and his setting[49]," when man looks at life
without illusions, without hope, with a feeling of alienation. To
Sartre, it is looking into the heart of nothingness. To Camus, it is
the point where one realizes the habit that is living, realizes the
absence of any higher reason behind existence, suffering, and all
the agitations of daily life. We learn to live because before we
can realize we exist, we have already grown accustomed to it,
grown the habit of existing, assumed social roles, and learned
the rules of time.

But the absurdity of existence has more to it than that. We do
not necessarily assume the struggles of life because we make a
habit of it, although certainly habit does facilitate life, but rather
our innate instincts bred the habit into us. The absurdity comes
from being incarcerated by those archaic instincts, while knowing freedom through our cognizant conscious. It is bitterly ironic
that the instincts that have given us the ability to understand the
concepts of free will, immortality, and meaning, through the
power of abstraction, have also denied those exact concepts to
us.

My will is not entirely free in the sense that I cannot act
irrespective of the situation and its circumstances. In not being
privy to the underlying rules that the instincts set out for me, I am
in a sense a prisoner to them. All my, and anybody else's, behavior is acted out according to the adaptation of experience by the
instincts. Thus my will is not completely free, but constrained
according to the objectives laid out by my instincts. However,
this does not mean that my behavior is deterministic, either. Absolutely determining or predicting somebody's behavior is impossible, even if we could someday map out all the instincts.
Merely considering the infinite possible ways to interpret any
experience or situation, and considering the infinite degrees of

---

[49] Albert Camus, *Myth of Sisyphus*

possible instinct intensities with which a person is born or develops, makes predetermination an impossibility. The will is constrained, but within those constraints it has an infinite range of movement.

My will is no freer, and my life has no more meaning, than that of any other animal; but the difference is that I can understand, and desire, those concepts, unlike other animals. Therein lies the absurdity in the Faustian contract we have entered to gain our intelligence. We have gained cognizant intelligence, only to realize its limitations, and its temporality.

Habit is the easy way to live, but regardless of whether the habit exists or not, our innate directive to live would have to manifest itself this, or another, way. We cannot escape our instinct to live, but we can fight its manifestation as habit, and reinvent our existence through alternate manifestations. Do I eat at eight, twelve, and seven because it is habit, or do I eat because I see a purpose in it, and do I choose the food, the methods, and the times I eat with a purpose in mind?

There is nothing wrong with habit, however. Habit may be what we want, for whatever reason, be it comfort or happiness, for example. But time forces an imperative that obligates us to choose, be it habit or something else. I will discuss this imperative later in this chapter, but the following sections will deal with the theistic choices that society has thrust on us as an answer to the absurdity with which our instincts have presented us.

Living Pragmatically

There can *be* no difference anywhere that doesn't *make* a difference elsewhere-no difference in abstract truth that doesn't express itself in a difference in concrete fact and in conduct consequent upon that fact, imposed on somebody, somehow, somewhere and somewhen. The whole function of philosophy ought to

> be to find out what definite difference it will make to
> you and me, at definite instants in our life, if this world-
> formula or that world-formula be the true one.
>
> William James

Although the theories in this book are largely formed from
an eclectic mix of European and American philosophies, at their
heart is the American philosophy of Pragmatism. In fact the aim
of this book is to present the teachings of the modern philosophers through a Pragmatic lens. This exercise is performed to
extricate the relevance that these philosophies have to contemporary society, especially in light of the advances in medicine
and technology.

Charles Sanders Peirce first started the philosophical school
of Pragmatism and William James[50] and John Dewey[51] then advanced it in the early part of this century. Disenchanted with the
theoretical nature of European philosophy and their solipsistic
focus, the Pragmatists broke away with a mundane paradigm.
They argued that instead of theorizing about non-practical metaphysical issues such as the basis of perception and the nature of
the relationships between mind and matter, philosophers should
instead concentrate on issues and paradigms that serve to change
or affect human experience, as was first introduced by Peirce.
James took this a step forward and declared theories relevant if
they altered the basis of truth.

Peirce's version of pragmatism begins with the notion that a
person's beliefs are the basis for his actions and behavior. A
person's belief system is the set of standards, principles, and rules
by which he will act and lead his life, and the principles by which
he will judge other's actions and behaviors. Thus, the ultimate
meaning and importance of a thought or notion is the conduct

---

[50] William James, a popular philosopher and psychologist, was also well
known for authoring the popular Psychology textbook *Principles of Psychology* (1890)

[51] John Dewey, although an influential proponent of pragmatism, was
mostly devoted to the philosophy of education.

it elicits; the actions it produces is its significance. Notions and ideas are then inherently judged according to the implicit conduct they elicit. Phenomena are judged according to the impact they have on the practical world, and the effectual difference they make on other phenomena, objects, and people. The notions of "good" and "bad" can be allotted according to whether the practical impact of an idea or phenomenon is ultimately positive or negative, beneficial or detrimental, pleasurable or painful.

Although obvious as the philosophy seems, the repercussions of viewing the world and its phenomena in a Pragmatic viewpoint are vast. It grounds certain sets of abstractions such as art and metaphysics to a method of judgement, and it brings accountability to belief systems and behavior. When all phenomena are put under the Pragmatic microscope they are forced to account for their worth. Later in this chapter I will apply this notion more concretely. I will put modern philosophy and theology in general under the Pragmatic microscope. No longer will things be able to exist for their own sake, they must now serve a purpose under the sun.

Peirce's notion of pragmatism, however, is distinct from James'. James went further with the philosophy and incorporated the notion of truth, much to Peirce's disapproval. In James' words:

> " . . . truth is one species of good, and not as is usually supposed, a category distinct from good, and coordinate with it. The true is the name of whatever proves itself to be good in the way of belief, and good, too, for definite, assignable reasons . . . [Pragmatism's] only test of probable truth is what works best in the way of leading us, what fits every part of life best and combines with the collectivity of experience's demands, nothing being omitted."

Thus James redefined the notion of truth, an abstract human construction, by using another abstract human construction, "good." As far as definitions go, James' definition of truth is the most pragmatic and functional of any other in print. He attempted to ground truth with pragmatic practicality. James wanted a word to unify and represent the pragmatic ideal, to put it all together concisely. Thus he chose truth to be the unified representation of Pragmatic judgement. If something, by implementation, was practical and good, then by all useful purposes it was true. What matters is the outcome, the "cash-value" of a phenomenon. As long as the cash-value and effects of a certain conception or phenomenon was good, it was in the best interest of humanity for that to be considered true.

James realized that the notion of truth was a human concoction for the sake of easy communication, and thus attempted to replace its abstract definition with a utilitarian one[52]. Unfortunately, regardless of whether the definition for truth is abstract or utilitarian, the concept remains fleeting because it is concocted.

---

[52] I am talking about subjective, or in Kantian terms, synthetical, truth here, not apodictic or analytical truth. Synthetical truth is relative, empirical, and subject-dependent, while analytical truth is comprised of man-made statements or definitions that are necessarily true because they are man-made. Analytical truths have no content to add to experience. For example, an eye-witness account is a synthetical truth, while the fact that "marriage" includes the sharing of vows is true by definition since that is how we have defined marriage, and is thus analytical. To take the concept a little deeper, math is both synthetical and analytical. The building blocks of math, "1+1=2" for example, are synthetical in that they are derived from our experience with our surroundings. 1+1=2 is derived from the concept that AN apple is ONE apple, another, different apple is also ONE apple, but put together they are TWO apples. But these building blocks have also been used to derive abstract mathematical concepts. 1/0, imaginary numbers, and infinity are all abstract concepts without empirical grounding and thus analytical by nature. They are place holders in equations that make things balance, known and defined by a bunch of symbols. We can experience the synthetical ONE apple, but we cannot experience the analytical 1i apple.

Truth is an abstraction that cannot be grounded because it seeks to describe something that is subject dependent-and relativistic (more on this subject later). By shifting its focus to that which is "good," James is replacing one abstraction with another. As difficult as truth is to bound, "good" and "bad" are even worse. How do we judge goodness, and then how do we hold that universally? What is good and what is bad? And therefore, what is true and what is false? These question have no answers, and truth has no grounding.

As instrumental as James was to the proliferation of Pragmatism and psychology, I have to agree with Pierce and discount James foray into truth. I've introduced the concept because of James' importance, and will let the reader make up his own mind on which school of thought to adopt, if at all. But for the sake of this books' discussion, I will mostly adapt Pierce's interpretation.

Chapter 9.

Theism: Knowing How to Choose

A Basis for Religious Orders

Through the ages man has demonstrated an inherent proclivity towards seeking divine explanations to those things without scientific rationale. All cultures have their gods, creation legends, ghosts, or souls to explain internal and external phenomena outside scientific proof. The Scandinavian region had Odin and his brethren of gods, the Mediterranean was rife with pagan, Christian, Muslim, and others, the Indians had Hinduism and Buddhism, also among a multitude of other religions, the Africans and American Indians had pagan gods, and so on across cultures and times. These gods and divine beliefs, as Nietzsche would say, not only helped justify existence, they also gave justification to unexplainable pain and suffering, as well as pleasure. Suffering, not only that of existence, but also that from accidents, natural events, and human infliction, is easier to endure when it serves a purpose, whether the supposed expiation of sins, or the obtaining of rewards. When hurricanes tear our homes apart, the associated pain is more endurable when we believe that our behaviors caused it, or that the pain is a means to obtaining rewards. The pain is then justified. Similarly, good fortune is better relished when the fortune is believed to be deserved or bestowed, rather than having to deal with the guilt of simple serendipity.

Along with their justification, mysticism also personifies unexplainable phenomena to allow man to displace feelings and emotions against them. Hating a storm is easier if it is personified by an evil deity, allowing the victims to vent frustration and anger that otherwise would have no outlet. Making sacrifices for good weather is also mollifying when the weather is personified by a helpful deity, rather than having to sit and wait. Waiting is frustrating, while working toward something is rewarding.

The benefits of justifying suffering and pleasure are obviously the abatement of anguish and guilt, respectively. Many times a family or person is trapped in desperate situations, for example where a person is terminally ill, or an elderly couple is mired in poverty without means of improvement. Religion is a worthy means of instituting meaning, hope, and respite from earthly problems. Lying on a deathbed, religion gives a person something to look forward to in an afterlife, distracts that person from pain, and makes the pain meaningful and thus easier to bear. As Marx put it, religion is the opiate of the masses.

However, such sentiment does have marked drawbacks. Giving divine reasons to predicaments takes away personal accountability and responsibility for those predicaments. Accepting a fate is far easier when it is consecrated as divine, considering the difficulty in arguing with an omnipotent and omniscient being. Fighting fate could practically be considered fighting the gods, truly a losing battle, a rationale that instead leads to an abnegation of responsibility. Justifying doing anything at all becomes difficult since fighting the gods is a losing battle; or similarly, it makes failure easier to bear, and harder to fight. Also, giving predicaments a divine reason absolves people of blame since they are mere puppets under divine hands, removing accountability (e.g., the influence of evils spirits such as Satan). Absolving oneself with holy water is easier than facing and dealing with causes and consequences. This is liberating when in situations without hope or reprieve. Anything done to ease suffering during situations without mitigating recourses is commendable.

However, it is binding in situations where change is possible. When people no longer see themselves able to completely influence and alter the future, and when they are no longer able to completely suffer the consequences, then they are no longer free. Their hands are now tied by the images of their gods. They are no longer completely free to act when they feel that they are being watched at every turn. They are no longer completely free to act when the gods influence their actions. Regardless of the Christian Bible stating that "God helps those who help themselves," divine influence still has a mollifying effect. However slight this mollifying effect might be, the result is that the desire and need to act is not as strong. Pain and anguish developed in man and beast as a way to incite a reaction. When that pain and anguish is attenuated, the response is lessened by degrees.

It comes to be that divine belief has both favorable and unfavorable characteristics depending on the situation. Bringing this back to our discussion on freedom, power lies in being able to choose. While freedom bears anguish and security bears bliss, a better chance of fulfillment can be had through the former. The issue of theism and freedom, along with man's ability to choose, will be discussed in this chapter. Many people doubt whether man can choose to have faith or not, but hopefully by the end of this book I will have convinced those people otherwise.

The Choice of Theism

Ultimately, being religious or theistic is a major choice in life. Whether to interpret the events of life as divine or random in nature, or to interpret ancient writings as theistic versus literary, is a choice we all make. There is no proof one way or the other, no certainty, only probabilities. Therefore being theistic, versus agnostic, versus atheistic, is a choice, fraught with consequences and repercussions. William James did not believe we had a choice; that the decision was made passionately and intuitively despite reason. We either have faith rooted in our passions, or we do not. James is right, but to a degree. Yes, belief comes from will, intuition, and passion, but intuition and passion are not something we are born with *a priori* and irrevocably. They are not something hidden and protected deep in the recesses of the mind. Intuition and passion are things in constant flux, changing and adapting, influenced both by experience and intellect. We have discussed several methods of changing our intuitions, passions, and wills. For example, we discussed rebuilding belief structures by making the base assumptions transparent, and challenging them logically. Through self inculcation of base assumptions we can build a belief structure. This self inculcation can involve simple logical analysis, to self immersion in environments favorable to the belief of the desired set of assumptions. Since reality is relative and subjective, nothing stops us from changing our minds. Related to that, we also discussed influencing our will by creating domino chains according to the experiences within which we immerse ourselves.

Regardless of how we create options, the choice of theism is an imperative of the self-preservation instinct. The instinct gives rise to the passion for life, which provides the basis upon which people feel the need to give meaning to life. The choice is whether to embed that meaning solely within the temporal context of an individual's impact on himself and society, or to include the context of the divine. Both choices have positive and negative repercussions.

Take the case of a man crossing a high wire hundreds of feet up in the air at the circus. The man has to get from one circus post to the next by crossing a wire several floors up, with only the help of a balancing pole. If that circus performer crosses the high wire with a safety net underneath, he faces less risk of major injury or death, and thus his fear of crossing is lessened, his concentration less intense, his attention less heightened, and the sense of victory and satisfaction at having crossed the wire is minimized since less was at risk. In attempting the feat he only needs to fear humiliation and perhaps losing his job since the net would save him if he fell. However, if he crosses the wire without a net, every step he takes could be his last. Such fear of death ensures his devoted concentration and focus every second he's on that wire, intensifies the whole experience, and proves to be a far more rewarding feat to accomplish if successful. How markedly different his celebration would be at crossing the wire if his life was spared, versus if he crossed it and merely spared himself the humiliation of falling. Thus Camus' statement that "Living an experience, a particular fate, is accepting it fully."

Similarly, how much more marked would life be when every second, every experience, is one among a few? If all we have are those seventy years of life given to us, then how precious are each of those years if there is nothing else? How can we appreciate anything if we seriously believed that an eternity followed it? How could we appreciate any one second or any one experience if we knew that an infinite number of them followed? Some people might answer that we can appreciate them because they are the only moments we have like them since we are on earth only once, and the life that follows death is nothing like that that preceded it. But we do not know what form an existence outside of life on earth would take, and therefore we would have to imagine that it would be like our mortal life since that is the only basis upon which we can imagine. If we had to believe in an existence outside of mortal life, we would have to imagine it taking the same form because we would know of no other, and any other form would be incomprehensible. If life after death were essentially different from life before death, then it would be incomprehensible to us during our mortal life, and tying it back to our current existence would be impossible and immaterial. If the existence that follows mortal life is incomprehensible to us while in mortal form, then it is a moot subject. We do not have the language to discuss it, the mental concepts to visualize it, or the capacity to affect it or be affected by it. We could not act or think about it, and therefore its existence to us would be nullified.

In effect, theism mollifies the first instinct and its manifested passion for life and fear of death. Theism was created as a response to the first instinct since its existence prompted the need for meaning, thus it follows that theism serves the purpose of mollifying that which created it, the self-preservation instinct. As a safety net, theism relieves the pressure of living an ephemeral and ultimately meaningless existence, but as a direct consequence it also assuages man's passion for life. Life is most valuable and intense when it is shortest lived, thus extending it or broadening its secular scope will consequently diminish its intensity and value, and thus man's passion for it. We would cherish eating a certain fruit more if we knew it was the last of its kind we would taste, versus the limited enjoyment we get from eating the hundredth apple from a lifetime consumption of one thousand apples. Similarly, we would value life's experiences more if we felt that they held purely an intrinsic value and that they were limited in number, versus tying the value of an experience to an extrinsic source and believing that the experience was insignificant among an eternity of them. Thus, passion for life is the price of theism, and the self-preservation instinct the captive.

But theism would not be much of a choice unless it also had beneficial effects; a price to pay for choosing atheism or agnosticism. That price is passion for death. The man on the high-wire act, although focused, attentive, and passionate, is also scared, nervous, and stressed out. He is so concentrated with the task at hand that he hardly has the ability to notice the audience applauding, or the performances of the other circus performers. He has no hope of survival if he falls.

Similarly, the atheist has no hope for surviving. He is tortured by the seeming meaninglessness and tragedy of life, and he suffers because life is short. Slowing down and enjoying idle time is more difficult to do. His fears and his sufferings are intensified, lacking justification or sense of justice in life. The theist, on the other hand, finds hope in his deity, he lives with the expectation of divine justice, and all acts and events have extrinsic meaning. For the theist, suffering is acceptable, and more bearable, since it has higher meaning. In the light of higher meaning and infinite time, stopping to smell the roses becomes second nature.

In essence, the choice is between the life of high peaks and low valleys inherent in atheism, or the temperate life of theism. A choice between passion and dread, and happiness and justifiable suffering. A choice born of instinct, neither is wrong and neither is right. Western man no longer lives in a jungle of threatening animals and constant starvation, he now lives in a world where food is a temptation and the only threatening animal is the occasional flu. Perhaps the passion for life has become more vestigial than necessary. As technology endows us more and more with leisure time, and the necessities of life become more automatic and easier to acquire, the self-preservation instinct in turn becomes more of a vestigial luxury. As such, the choice of theism is also a luxury of life, but a far-reaching and encompassing choice at that. Choosing is an imperative of time, but neither choice is right nor wrong.

Pascal's Wager

The following question then has to be posed: If atheism or agnosticism is chosen and life lacks any discernible divine meaning, any superbeings to give it a cause, any afterlife to give it a direction—then what is the point of living it? What is the point of creating and reaching goals? How can we justify the constant laboring and suffering associated with life? The answer to all the questions is "None." Life has no point but life itself. Laboring and suffering lack any meaning but the fruits they yield. But then, what happiness can be derived from an existence without reason? The ecstasy of life itself is what can be derived from it, for only when we chance to lose it all can we appreciate what we have.

As Camus puts it:

> "It now becomes clear, on the contrary, that [life] will be lived all the better if it has no meaning. Living an experience, a particular fate, is accepting it fully. Now, no one will live this fate, knowing it to be absurd, unless he does everything to keep before him that absurdity brought to light by consciousness . . . Living is keeping the absurd alive. Keeping it alive is, above all, contemplating it . . . One of the only coherent philosophical positions is thus revolt . . . Just as danger provided man the unique opportunity of seizing awareness, so metaphysical revolt extends awareness of the whole experience. It is that constant presence of man in his own eyes. It is not aspiration, for it is devoid of hope. That revolt is the certainty of a crushing fate, without the resignation that ought to accompany it."

In other words, for Camus life is not about escaping its own brutality through hope, faith, or meaning, but about facing it squarely in the eyes, and fighting it, revolting, feeling life as one feels a rush of adrenaline, through the revolt.

For illustrative purposes, let's consider Pascal's wager. Pascal, the renowned mathematician and Christian philosopher, postulated that believing in God was the rational thing to do. He asserted that believing in God implied the possibility of eternal salvation, as described by Christian gospel. If this God exists and you believe in him and follow the gospel of his son Jesus, then you will go to heaven and exist in peace and harmony. On the other hand, if you did not believe in him or did not follow the gospel of Jesus, then you forfeited those benefits, or worse, you moved on to an existence of eternal damnation. So according to Pascal, choosing between faith and not believing is a loaded wager. You either believe in God and take the chance of going to heaven, or you do not believe in God and risk nothing, or risk worse by going to hell. By having faith you have much to gain if God exists, but gain nothing or worse if you don't have faith. However, if God does not exist, you lose nothing by having faith, and you gain nothing by not having faith. To Pascal the wager was obviously loaded in favor of faith since you could only gain with faith, and only lose in not believing. Either believe in God and possibly win eternal salvation, or not believe and possibly go to eternal damnation.

He rationalized that understanding God in human terms was both impossible and unnecessary, but having faith was enough. To him the concept of God was similar to infinity, impossible to grasp, but existent nonetheless.

Pascal's wager has many shortcomings that nullify it. One of the most convincing is the argument that challenges Pascal's assumption that the Christian description of God is true, that believing in Him implied Salvation. The truth may be the opposite, that God saves the unbeliever and punishes the believer. Like Pascal said, as we cannot comprehend the concept of infinity, we cannot comprehend God, and therefore would have no clue as to what His rules of existence might truly be. Perhaps God rewards the theistic nonconformist, the nonbeliever, and punishes the theistic conformist, or the believer. That would stand Pascal's wager on its head and make not believing the loaded choice. Believing in Pascal's assumption is no more rational than believing in its opposite, that God rewards one type of person versus another. Pascal, being Christian, would understandably start with the Bible as his assumption base. But he cannot make the assumption that a non-Christian would start there, too. In fact, any argument he uses to proselytize cannot use any gospel as an assumption base since by definition a nonbeliever does not believe in the Bible and its contents, and therefore does not adhere to its assumptions. Pascal would first have to convince us that if a God existed that the God would be the God of the Christians, and that his description in the Bible is accurate. Then his wager would hold water.

Pascal's wager, though, has not been introduced here so we can play devil's advocate, but rather to introduce an argument more pertinent to moral freedom and finding a point to living. I challenge Pascal's other assumption. Pascal assumed wrongly that nothing was risked in believing in God. As we now know, there are no free lunches. Any gain will always imply a risk or a loss; sometimes the challenge is in finding what you give up in risking. Pascal lost sight of this.

Following an organized religion, separate from the tradeoffs implicit in theism that have been already discussed, involves believing or following a number of religious principles, ideals, and traditions. The short of these are moral and ethical commandments, masses, and holiday rituals. The long of these are sexual practices, dietary practices, confessions, plus more. What we give up with some of these is obvious. By following the guidelines for dietary practices, for example not eating red meat during certain times, we give up a freedom of choice in eating. With sexual guidelines we give up the freedom of choosing when and how to interact sexually, as well as severely influencing the direction our lives take in certain situations, such as unwanted pregnancies. Whether or not a couple chooses to abort will dramatically alter the course of many lives. Any factors used in making the decision can be considered as risking the possibility of making a more suitable choice. Choosing to follow a certain religion will severely influence the course of a person's life, risking the possibility of another course being a more suitable one.

However, we do not have to be Roman Catholics, Hassidic Jews, Janists, Sikhs or any other form of strict religious followers to be bound by religion. Simply following the moral and ethical commandments outlined by any religious text constitutes greater liberties through less freedom. Although some would argue that liberties and freedoms are synonymous, they can at times be antithetical. Following a set of commandments is liberating in that it moves accountability from an individual person to an entire society. We are no longer burdened with the freedom of choosing paths depending on the pertinent circumstances if the paths have already been outlined, or chosen, for us. We are no longer saddled with the burden of the risks of making regrettable choices. Liberty lies in reducing choices, and therefore reducing burdens, stress, and also accountability and personal risk. Although our liberties are increased, we also would no longer have the freedom to weigh the benefits of every decision against the detriments, and stress over the decision and its effects. Instead, we make decisions based on whether things are considered "good" or "bad" by the moral codes dictated by religion. The effects are thus ruled "good" or "bad" based on whether we followed the letter of the defined guidelines. Therefore, we are now liberated from having to be personally accountable for the effects of our actions. As long as what we do is "right" or "good," the outcomes are virtually inconsequential, and therefore non-stressing. With religion choice is bounded and liberty increased, but at the expense of freedom. With its opposite, freedom of morality, we are completely accountable for all effects, and therefore must analyze each decision based on both the desirability of the actions and their effects. Stress, pain, and work is added, but freedom is increased.

Some would argue that we are still just as free and have the same choices under religious doctrine than under none, but instead merely choose to go with those stated in religious gospel. This is self-defeating logic, however, if we truly have faith. Either we have true faith and follow the commandments of the religion, or we doubt and are not true believers. Having the freedom to choose implies having doubt in religious gospel and the religion itself, otherwise we would have unquestioning faith. Unquestioning faith implies just that, following the letter of the religion without questioning it. If you cannot question the basis on which to make your decision, then you do not have choice. If you truly believed in an omniscient and all-powerful God that created a set of immutable commandments, you would not and could not go against his commandments for fear of imminent retribution or punishment. You would not have the ability to choose from multiple possibilities since those possibilities are bounded and categorized by religion.

For example, according to many religions, stealing is never an option. It goes against gospel and assures punishment, especially if an omniscient god knew of the perpetration of the act. Therefore, choice is bounded, and the freedom to steal denied. If a devout follower where to steal, then *either he has accepted his fate of divine punishment, or he doubts the principles of his religion.* If he accepts his fate of punishment, then he will live a life of fear of the afterlife, fear of his god, guilt of abandoning his religion's morals, and shame in the eye of his fellow believers. This is not freedom. This is an internal sentence, an internal jail far worse than a physical one.

I'm not stipulating that stealing is a good thing, but I'm not defining it as bad, either. Stealing is an act with consequences, some beneficial and some detrimental. We should weigh those consequences, and based on the outcomes decide whether stealing something at some point in time is more beneficial than not. For most circumstances, the detriment to the victim, the risk of being caught, and the increment in anarchy and lawlessness is not worth the slight and ephemeral gain of wealth. And thus stealing *should* become rare because it is detrimental to the individual and society in net, not because someone or something has ruled it as "bad." Freedom is to act based on circumstances and consequences, not on preordained rules of conduct and fear of divine retribution. The rules and the fear are irrelevant to pragmatic matters, and thus impinge on practical freedom.

All About Tradeoffs

Making choices always implies making tradeoffs between options, and religion is no different. There are many different religions from which to choose, with many different types and levels of beliefs, not to mention the many spiritual and non-organized belief systems external to them. What religion or what belief system is followed, and then to what extent, are all choices bearing tradeoffs. In the previous subchapter we discussed the strictly devout, but people who believe in organized religion superficially but doubt internally are also common. These people are engaging in serious self-deception. They are superficially making choices and following paths in which they do not believe. Ultimately, a life led by self-deception cannot be satisfying. At the slightest, such a person is wasting precious time in masses and events in which he does not believe. At its worst, the person is choosing careers, life partners, and teaching his children, among other things, based on false principles, ultimately leading to bitterness and disappointment.

In addition are those who believe in a god and an afterlife, but not the scriptures and traditions of an organized religion. They believe in the existence of a god, but not necessarily one described by any one religion, and therefore are not bounded by any set of moral codes of conduct or traditions. But still the world lacks free lunches. As liberating as is believing in an afterlife, a price still has to be paid for having the hope of salvation and the comfort of a higher being. That price is the previously described safety net that theism provides in mortal life. It is the attenuation of the self-preservation instinct, dampening both the passions for life and death. For some, that is a high price to pay; for others, that is a desirable effect. Theism is a tradeoff, and anybody that regards it as a panacea is deluding himself.

Believing in an afterlife also bears a danger. That danger is the risk of allowing the belief to pervade life's choices and decisions. The afterlife, being foreign and unknowable, cannot influence nor be *discernibly* influenced by temporal life. To believe otherwise is to bias life's decisions and choices by an irrelevancy, risking suboptimal decisions.

To draw upon Pragmatic thought, our existence is bound to our mortal life, period. Pondering those things lacking a basis of comparison or analysis in practical life is pointless. We cannot theorize or act on those things outside the realm of our experience and understanding, and therefore they must be considered non-existent. Those things that do not affect us and cannot be affected by us in any discernible fashion are for all rational purposes non-existent to us.

Imagine a rock that exists in another universe, a rock that we will never have any contact with it nor it with us; not even light emanating from our sun could reach it. We cannot affect it, it cannot affect us Not even gravity ties us together. Would there be any purpose in thinking of this rock, imagining it, theorizing about it, or having absolutely anything at all to do with it? For practical purposes this rock does not exist, has not existed, and will never exist. Until we discover a way to communicate with other universes, if they exist, this rock will have no impact or bearing on our life, and we will have no impact or bearing on its existence, regardless of what we think or do.

The only discernible impact a rock in another universe has on us is our capacity to imagine it. We imagine it, we give it characteristics, and it is only through our imagination that we are affected. But it is not the rock itself that affects us. It is purely the images of it which we have created in our minds that affects us. That rock's actual existence is irrelevant to what we do or do not imagine. As such, thinking of this rock is purely our choice, letting its imaginary existence affect us. The rock itself has no bearing, and therefore does not practically exist.

The existence of an afterlife is like that rock—irrelevant in that it cannot affect us nor us it in any way we can discern, and therefore non-existent. People will argue that we can affect it, but this argument lacks any basis for proof, nothing to sway us one way or another as to whether this is true or not. However, herein lies a power for us to choose to believe in it or not, for those mental creations will affect us, both with benefits and detriments. But to choose wisely we should know ahead of time of those benefits and detriments of believing. To excuse having faith in the afterlife by saying that life after death is unlike life before death in a fashion incomprehensible to us and thus outside the realm of proof is exactly the same as saying that for all practical purposes, that life after death does not exist in any practical fashion. Giving life after death credence through the excuse of incomprehensibility is self-deceiving, for its existence is irrelevant regardless of human comprehension. It is another learning from Schroedinger's Cat.

As long as Schroedinger's cat's status is indefinable, its status is also unknown. We cannot act based on the cat's status as long as we cannot define it. The rock, as life after death, are akin to the cat's status; indefinable, unknowable, and therefore, impossible upon which to base any actions. But in Schroedinger's example, Schroedinger knew that the cat existed, and therefore could pin down that the cat was a mixture of alive and dead. In the case of an afterlife, we have absolutely no basis upon which to state any assumptions of what it consists. The whole concept is indefinable and irrelevant. It is a rock in another universe.

So all that we have left to say about life after death is that it must be like life before death in order for it to be of any relevance. But with what proof can we assert this statement? If life after death is like that before it, then it must have some practical proof that would be comprehensible to us since the two existences have similarities. But none exists. Nothing in man's existence points to a reasonably probable afterlife. But if the afterlife had a proof, then all that would say is that our mortal lives would be essentially worthless in light of the fact that there would be another to follow it. In other words, how could we value our time here if we knew that it was dispensable? We are lucky that our life is short, and nonrecurring.

Life is precious because it is ephemeral and singular in occurrence, but it is also precious because it is devoid of meaning.
Once we attribute a meaning, such as an afterlife, to life, it becomes merely a means to an end, rather than being an end in-
and-of-itself. When we attribute a meaning to life, we bind ourselves by the walls of that meaning. We no longer live life for the
sake of its own pleasure and reward, but for the sake of its meaning. Life becomes a trip to somewhere, where we merely look at
the scenery because it is something to do while we wait to get to
our destination, rather than life being the destination itself where
we get off and take in everything there. What is the point of a
trip? Its destination. What is the point of the destination? Nothing other than the destination itself. Which of the two do we
remember the most, which do we cherish more? The destination, of course. To stand Pascal's Wager on its head, if life has a
possibility of being all that there is and all that we have, then why
take the chance of making it the trip to a destination, rather than
the destination itself? Why attribute a meaning to life or a reason
to it, and make it a trip, when we could be chancing being wrong?
The question should not be, "What is the meaning of life?" but
rather, "Why should life have meaning?"

If life is all that exists then it is its own destination. We are
going nowhere else from here, therefore make the most of it
while we can. Making an itinerary of all the places we want to
see, and giving a purpose to the trip, will ensure that we don't
waste time walking around aimlessly. Although at times we will
be aimless because we don't have the background to formulate
an itinerary, the aimlessness will be temporary until we stumble
upon something of importance that helps us move forward.

Thus believing in a god and afterlife of no denomination
bears several prices, prices which must be considered against the
more obvious rewards of faith. Those rewards, being the practical and temporal effects of the belief upon our consciousness,
are not the effects that we believe are had in the afterlife. The
prices, on the other hand, boil down to a compromised valua-

tion of life and time, a life and time that may be singular in
importance, and thus infinite in value.

Then there are those who believe in some form of deity, but
not in an afterlife (commonly referring to themselves as being
spiritual but not religious). To them the benefits of a faith lie in
the companionship and meaning offered by a being that is always present. But a price still exists. Social psychology has demonstrated that people behave in dissimilar fashions depending
on whether they believe they are alone or not. This is so obvious
we don't need social psychology to tell it to us. We do things
when we are alone that we would never imagine doing with
other people around, such as being naked, for example. It is not
a far cry to extend this reasoning to conclude that believing in
the existence of a god that is always present and always watching
will affect the behavior of the believer. He might not do things
that he considers wrong, such as stealing, for fear of retribution,
or he might not do things that he considers embarrassing for fear
of mortification. The person might or might not commit these
acts, but his faith will regardless have an impact on the believer,
which results in the attenuation of the freedoms he allows himself, or in the freedoms he perceives to have. The believer will
not do certain things because of his belief, or if so, he does them
begrudgingly or with fear in his heart. Either way, he is held
captive by his belief.

De Facto Isolation and Mitigation

Whatever belief, doctrine, philosophy, or religion is chosen,
whether it is true as opposed to another is irrelevant. Truth has
no application in an existence where measurement is flawed by
definition and reality is bounded by sensual perceptions. There
is no such thing as truth, only probabilities, which is why arguing
the truth of one religious or philosophical concept over another
is an exercise in futility. The power lies not in the truth of the

religion or philosophy, but in the practical effects it has on a person's life. A religion or philosophy should be chosen on the basis of its repercussions in day-to-day life, and on the basis that its doctrines are most probable and most applicable, and not in the "truth" of its statements. We would hope that a person would pick the philosophy or religion most beneficial to him, and that others would respect that choice. As long as the philosophies of others do not impinge on our freedoms, we have to respect their choices. We have to assume their choices are the most fitting, and be happy for them.

Truth is flawed because everything as we experience it is imperfect since we are flawed. Everything that we experience we do so through our senses in route to perceiving it with our minds, senses which are flawed and biased. The mind, and therefore a person, is separated from his surroundings by a physical layer. In other words, the mind, which is an abstraction at a high level, and a series of bio-electrical reactions at its lowest level, must interact and communicate with its surroundings, which are physical in nature. Thus, a degree of separation exists between a person and his surroundings—the separation of mind and matter. That separation is manifest in the five senses: sight, taste, smell, sound, and touch.

In Chapter Seven we discovered that we can never truly experience those objects around us. To truly know and understand what it means to be a table, we need to have been a table. Otherwise we are forced to understand the concept of "table" by its physical characteristics: dimensions, smell, taste, surface roughness, heat conductivity, etc. Our minds are in one world, and our surroundings in another one, another dimension. And the connection or window between the two is physical interpretation. What does it mean to be a table? We'll never know; but we do know what a table looks, sounds, smells, tastes, and feels like. Whatever occurs in that environment, and whatever objects exist, can be witnessed or felt through this bio-electrical layer that interprets the environment into a form digestible by the mind.

The bio-electrical layer starts with physical organs, is translated into electrical signals by the body, and is perceived by the mind as the manifestation of the environment through the five senses. If a rock is present in our environment, we perceive it because we can see it, hear it, touch it, smell it, and taste it. The rock's presence is evinced through our senses.

We only know what it is to be ourselves, and we are alone in that world and dimension where our minds reside. Alone behind our interpretations, only we know what it means to be ourselves and what we experience. We can try to communicate ourselves with others, but our attempts will always be limited—bound by bio-electrical interpretations and bio-physical communication. Thus we are ultimately alone, and thus, we are ultimately lonely.

This is exacerbated by the fact that we are constantly trying to substantiate our experiences through social validation. Trapped in a subjective and external reference-frame-free world, the more we can validate an experience, the more "real" it seems. But in the end, it is impossible to validate whether our bio-electrical interpretations of the environment are accurate or flawed since we can only seek validation through the same interpretive system we are seeking to validate. In other words, it is impossible to determine if a thermometer was off if all we could use to gauge temperature was the same thermometer we were trying to calibrate. If it read the room temperature as being eighty degrees Fahrenheit, without another thermometer to calibrate the first we would have to take the temperature as gospel, without knowing if it actually were eighty-two or seventy-eight degrees. Our senses *are* that thermometer. We take what they transmit to us as gospel because we have no other set of senses to calibrate against. We can use one sense to somewhat gauge the others, but it's a crude check. For example, we can check if something we see is actually there by touching it, but we can't determine if the color or opaqueness of the object at hand is what we see. This exacerbates the feeling of isolation since we're trapped behind and dependent upon this interpretive system that is impossible to validate.

It is a painful existence, one of unmitigated loneliness. We try to mitigate it by getting married and hopefully forming a bond that is deeper than the walls of physical limitations. But the walls of the physical world are not to be broken so easily, the incarceration and entrapment within them being immutable. Regardless of our attempts, we permanently reside behind the walls of bio-electrical interpretation. So being the creative beings that we are, we invent a different being that can transcend those physical limitations. Nothing says that we cannot; no proof denies the being his existence.

We imagine a being that knows everything about us. He knows everything that we have done, and everything that we intend to do. He knows our dreams, our fears, and our motivations. In essence, he knows us better than we know ourselves. We are no longer alone in our dimension. A god can visit us there, and keep us company. When things get frightening or difficult to handle, we can turn inward and talk to him. We are no longer alone in our world, having to face those internal and external battles without complete sympathy and understanding.

The effect is completely soothing. The sense of isolation is mollified, and in its stead are feelings of understanding and protection. Since it is created through folklore and imagination, a god is capable of filling whatever gaps exist in life. The effects upon the individual are deeply impacting, in some instances they are beneficial and in others deleterious.

As with all other emotions and human characteristics, the feeling of isolation may have evolutionary significance. The question that should be asked is whether this characteristic applies in modern society, or if it has become effectually vestigial. If it were vestigial, then its mitigation would be purely beneficial, for example like the removal of an ailing appendix. But experience proves that this is not the case.

As was discussed in previous chapters, humans are naturally

social animals, dependent on society for protection, for the passing of knowledge, for a means of reproduction. Our senses of isolation and loneliness thus play roles in securing this dependence. They are drivers toward getting us to socialize with our fellow brothers and sisters. These senses are in essence metaphysical sticks whipping us toward a desired behavior.

But as with some of the other manifestations of the instincts and human physiology, our sense of isolation can, and is, mollified through metaphysical means. Creating a being that provides understanding and companionship is mollifying, but at the price of abating the intended effect of driving man toward socialization. A god's companionship is also a double-edged sword that should be wielded with cognizance of its edges—the benefits of companionship, mitigation of pain, and ensuing liberty, versus capitulation of moral freedoms and increased apathy.

Critics might argue that religion has the opposite effect, uniting people under the umbrella of a common belief, providing the seed for socialization. That argument, however, lies outside the point that is being made. Religion in that sense is merely another type of social club, akin to golf clubs, card-playing clubs, and the like. In that context religion merely supplies a setting for the gathering of people with the goal of providing a social function. This social function proffers a carrot of enticement for members to participate, but its relation to a god is merely a pretext. The mitigation of isolation by a god's company is unrelated to the social benefits of organized religion.

Some people might also argue that the edges of the sword of religion are blunt, not very strong or intense, because the real reason behind a god is spiritual knowledge. For some people, the effects of religion are small, and for others large, running a gamut of intensity. But regardless of the intensity, the effects will exist, and those effects will have far-reaching repercussions in a person's life, repercussions that should be chosen, not blindly accepted.

Theism under the Pragmatic Microscope

However slightly possible, all things are still possible. Existence is such that any metaphysical explanation is probable and irrefutable. As was discussed previously, by existing we become active participants and will always influence the results of any observation, making it uncertain. We exist, therefore we influence our surroundings. By observing something, anything, with any one of our given senses, we influence or create some kind of change in that something we observe. When temperature is measured, for example, heat is exchanged with the object being measured, changing its temperature slightly. When a particle's position is measured, it's momentum is changed, precluding knowledge of its future path. Through measurement, we alter that something that we observe, adding a nuance of uncertainty. Therefore, everything that we know has been altered by our observation of it, making everything slightly uncertain and our measurements and observations slightly off. Everything in an inherently uncertain existence is possible.

Theism is a choice because anything is possible, because the manifestation of the instincts have become more luxury than necessity, allowing for their placation, and because the repercussions of the theistic choice are paradigmatic, and the choice of religion antithetical to the impetus of the instincts. The repercussions are so profound that the choice must be done openly and knowingly, otherwise condemning the individual to confusion and countering views, to lost time and lost energy. But the key is that the choice be paradigmatic, and not escapist.

Because we do not know anything for certain, anything is possible. However, for a theistic person to base his goals, thoughts, and actions solely on the virtue of divine reason is improvident. Acting based on things irrelevant to the situation and circumstances of the act, based on things slightly possible, is a tragedy. The tragedy lies in that we are only guaranteed to have that time we spend on earth, and to spend it on things that do not directly apply to the time past, present, and future spent alive, but on other things that divert our attention from the probable elements of our situation, is improvident. What we wind up escaping is exactly that which we only possess—which is time spent alive.

This is not to say that theism is illogical. Theism has its attributes, which to some may be considered more beneficial than detrimental. However, being theistic is different from using theism as a form of escapism. The tragedy lies in the latter, for all that is being escaped is life on earth, the only certainty. Escapism implies acting without a secular basis, without considering what the secular situations and consequences of a choice or an action are, and therefore escaping the worldly responsibility of those choices or actions. It is killing a doctor because of a sacrilegious abortion, it is being biased against a religious group, it is choosing a moral principle because it is written rather than because it makes sense, it is anything that is done counter to mundane sense for the sake of the divine. Escapism is committing an act blind to the consequences and situations on earth, based only on theistic reason. Praying, for example, is not escapist in light of its physical effects—that it reduces stress, soothes the mind, and institutes hope and tranquility.

The moment we turn solely toward the ethereal, independent of the secular, for goals and for fulfillment is the moment we have turned faith into blind faith. We cannot reach a goal that has no grounding on the temporal since we have no true way of affecting or influencing the outcome, or we have no way of assessing whether we have achieved our goal. For instance, if our goal is to gain admittance into a heaven by following a set of moral laws, then we have no way of assessing while on earth if we have achieved our goal. Our strict abidance to the letters of the law will be for naught during our lifetimes because we have no way of telling whether we gained admittance until we die. Not to mention that we don't know if there is a heaven to start with, if the moral sacraments spelled out in scriptures make any sense, or if there is anyone or thing keeping count. Any doubts that we have, which we must have as rational human beings, will spell out our frustration and unfulfillment. The fact of time is that it is short, and therefore should be spent on those things that impart the most positive, observable effects, based on a personal philosophy—whether theistic, agnostic, or atheistic by nature.

Chapter 10.

Putting it all together

The Interdependence of Freedom and Society

Since the Ancient Greeks, but most aptly explained in Thomas Hobbes' *Leviathan*, we have been dealing with the social polemic of the freedom paradox. This paradox seemingly arises when unlimited social freedom is granted to the individual, to the detriment and infringement of those around him. The more freedom is granted to the individual, we seem to think that more freedom is usurped from his neighbors, and ultimately the individual himself since we are all both individuals and neighbors. As freedom is increased on the one hand, it decreases on the other, in a seeming paradox. If Congress passed a law giving all citizens the freedom to steal with impunity, then as citizens we would all gain that freedom, but at the same time as neighbors we would all lose the freedom to possess things since everything is now essentially public domain. On the one hand we gain the freedom to *have* everything (by stealing it with impunity), and on the other we lose the freedom to own anything since anybody could steal it with the same impunity. As Hobbes puts it, during total, anarchistic freedom man develops a "per-petual and restless desire of power after power, that ceaseth only in death . . . In such condition, there is no place for industry; because the fruit thereof is uncertain . . . and which is worst of all, continual fear, and danger of violent death; and the life of man, solitary, poor, nasty, brutish, and short."

This is only a paradox on paper, however. The paradox as-sumes that given the opportunity to steal with impunity, any and all men would. In basic terms the assumption asserts that we are short-sighted and opportunistic beings, born without any inher-ent morality or sense of responsibility. Devoid of our own scruples and morals, we have to be taught and monitored by them. Thus, we have created a law forbidding stealing because otherwise an-archy would ensue. Proponents of these beliefs point to the Dark Ages shortly before Hobbes' time when anarchy was a way of life and man lived in relative squalor and misery. Wars, murders, rapes, and thievery were all a way of life. Contrast that to the U.S. today, and the differences speak for themselves, or so we would be led to believe. With all its rules and laws, the U.S. is a veritable utopia. A different picture exists, however. Compare any one of America's peaceful Native American tribes in pre-Columbian times with that of Stalin's Russia or Mao's China. The former had little in the way of laws, while the latter were chock full of them. Consequently, and in contrast to the para-dox, the former is a poster-child of natural freedom, while the latter two saw the execution, starvation, and murder of up to one hundred million people during peacetime. In other words, the former social structure had more social freedoms without the large decrease in personal freedoms assumed by the paradox; and the latter had fewer social freedoms without the increase in personal freedoms also assumed by the paradox. Clearly man is more complex than the assumptions taken by the freedom para-dox. Although I agree that overall man has less freedom through anarchy (or better put by Rousseau, he gains independence at the expense of civil freedom), it also follows that man tends toward a natural evolution of social integration without needing to force one. Again according to Rousseau, men can be both ruled and free as long as those rules are born of common, natural design, for a free man is one rules himself. When man instead forces a planned structure upon himself he runs into problems with myopic theories and blind assumptions over something so vastly complex as human social interaction. In Rousseau's words, "What makes the constitution of a state really strong and durable is such a close observance of conventions that natural relations and laws come to be in harmony on all points, so that the law, shall we say, seems only to ensure, accompany, and correct what is natural."

Many philosophies have been founded in response to the freedom paradox and its inherent assumptions. These more socialistic philosophies, such as those of Hegel, Mills, or Marx, seek to impose a social structure on the individual to exact humanitarian ideals upon him. These philosophies look at human society as being akin to an insect colony where the colony takes precedence over the individual. Those philosophers that espouse the more socialistic philosophies aim to maximize social utility rather than individual utility and thus may take the more individualistic existentialist philosophies introduced here as being somewhat anarchistic. As humanitarian as these philosophies aim to be in theory, in practice they prove to be impractical on one end of the spectrum, as is the case with Millsian Utilitarianism, and destructive on the other end, as has been the case with Marxism. The problem lies with the behavioral theories and assumptions that form the backbone of these philosophies, problems that result in the unnecessary infringement of an individual's freedoms.

First and foremost, the largest problem with socialist philosophies is the assumption that people are born devoid of morals and are exclusively opportunistic in their behavior. As an offshoot of the need for socialization by humans and other animals such as primates, evolution has developed the biology of empathy[53]. At its most simplistic, empathy is the recognition of emotions in other beings through sensorial cues such as body language, facial expressions, and sounds, that in turn trigger the reproduction of the implied emotions within the body of the observer. In other words, when we see other people act in such ways that it seems as though they were in pain, or perhaps pleasure, or sadness, or any other emotion, our brains automatically recognize the emotions and place the body and brain in the same states of emotion in order to empathize. Through this mechanism we can literally feel other people's emotions in order to create a response. If we know someone is in pain and we feel his pain, we become motivated to do something about it. When we do something about another's emotions we can then begin to form a friendship or begin a you-scratch-my-back-I'll-scratch-yours routine. Both of these social processes—friendship, and tit-for-tat—are essential in developing the social cohesion necessary for mutual survival.

Regardless, with or without social structures and moral codes, human beings are born with an ingrained sense of morality derived from the biologically programmed empathetic response[54]. People are not programmed to kill their neighbor at will, they are not programmed to steal chickens if given the chance, and they are not programmed to take advantage of everybody at every turn. They are in fact programmed to do the complete opposite; to feel their neighbor's pain so they can mollify it, and to feel their neighbor's happiness so they can rejoice in it. Jesus' message, stated numerous times and in numerous ways before

---

[53] Goleman, pg. 103-110

[54] According to Goleman, "The empathetic attitude is engaged again and again in moral judgements, for moral dilemmas involve potential victims... the roots of morality are to be found in empathy, since it is empathizing with the potential victims—someone in pain, danger, or deprivation, say—and so sharing their distress that moves people to act to help them. Beyond this immediate link between empathy and altruism in personal encounters, [Martin] Hoffman proposes that the capacity for empathetic affect, for putting oneself in another's place, leads people to follow certain moral principles."

and after him, "Do unto others as you would have them do unto you," comes not from the mind nor the heart, but from physiology. You do not need a socialist state to force people to take care of each other, you just need to give them the opportunity.

A second major problem with socialist philosophies is the notion of absolute rights and wrongs, or universal likes and dislikes (i.e. a universal template for "utility"). Although we have seen that we all indeed do have universal instincts, we have also seen that the application of those instincts according to experience and environment makes sweeping behavioral generalizations inappropriate. Thus, creating any philosophical framework based on social utility is difficult since the definition of utility is very subjective, and each individual will act based on his own background and environment. To try to fit one universal definition is futile at best.

Just as modeling human behavior in isolation from social influence is severely short-sighted, so is modeling society in isolation from the influences of its constituent individuals. The relationships between the two are so foundational and complex that thinking of the behavior of one without considering the influence of the other is impossible. All individuals are tied together by a need for survival and growth, a tie that provides the glue for society. Society is not an entity in its own sake, comprised of cells all dedicated to its survival, but instead an aggregation of individual entities, a virtual sum of Brownian fluid particles that when viewed at a distance take on the shape of its container. In a body, all cells are dedicated to the survival and benefit of the body. In a fluid, particles are held together by forces that attract them to each other, but they each are still completely independent of each other in their manner of existence, and the fluid takes on whatever shape or form is mandated by the environment. To understand a body, one must start at its characteristics as a whole, and tie its cells back to those characteristics. A red blood cell means nothing outside of its interactions with other cells in the body. To understand the characteristics of a fluid, one must go to the particles that comprise it, and to the forces that bind the individual particles together.

Rather than creating political and social philosophies that maximize social utility through the force-fitting of structures top-down, philosophies should theorize of maximizing social utility through the strengthening of the bonds between the individual and his collective neighbors, bonds collectively termed by Rousseau as the "general will." According to him, "it is what is common to those [private] different interests which yields the social bond; if there were no point on which separate interests coincided, then society could not conceivable exist. And it is precisely on the basis of this common interest that society must be governed." These common interests can only be common through nature or instinct since nurture and environment can only but differ by definition. Viewing these interests in terms of human instinctual drives is crucial when it comes to tapping into basic motivations, and in turn building social structures upon them. This is not necessarily hedonistic if one understands that society will explicitly thrive because it is in the individual's best interest, due to the individual's need for society to survive and flourish. According to Rousseau, all that results from the common general will, or common instinctual drives, by definition is "good," defining good and bad according to common social desire. The individual cannot survive without society and is thus dependent upon it, imputing an importance on society and its success in order for the individual to reap the fallout of growth, security, and wealth. To impose a structure that goes against the tide of instinctual motivation is fighting a losing battle, rather than strengthening a beneficial bond through explicit reinforcement. Imposing a structure places walls around natural individual freedoms—freedoms that are at the core of instinct satisfaction and fulfillment.

An example of imposition of a top-down structure versus the strengthening of bonds maybe the imposition of a tax aimed at redistributing wealth. The humanitarian cause of the top-down tax is egalitarianism; the method is a tax structure; and the results are tax evasion by those that feel the system is unfair, decreasing returns to work, resentment towards those that abuse the system, waste in the form of the bureaucracy that is now needed in monitoring and executing the law, some increased measure of egalitarianism as income is redistributed, and a decrease in freedom as now a certain portion of a person's working time and wages have been usurped by aggregate society. Examples of instinct reinforcement would be the creation of social awards recognizing charity and non-monetary rewards to volunteerism. These reinforcements promote charity through the tying of an individual's own sense of charity with his internal system of motivation. Since freedom is left intact in the form of choice, all the negative byproducts mentioned above are attenuated.

As far as the theory that the individual's best interest is served by a flourishing society, accumulation of wealth is not a zero-sum game, nor a linear function. In other words, I do not necessarily prosper merely at the expense of my neighbor, as is the case with a zero-sum situation. More often than not, I benefit mostly at a rate collinear with that of society in general. If I make three cars and my neighbor produces three tons of corn, we both benefit if we exchange a ton of corn for a car. One benefits because the other did, too, otherwise neither one would have bartered. My benefit benefits my neighbor. Respectively, society does not merely benefit linearly through the production of corn and cars. Cooperation allows society to benefit by more than just the sum of the corn and the car due to the interdependence of products and the decreasing utilities of consumption and wealth. Only when the corn is turned into ethyl alcohol does the car operate, but cooperation is necessary for this to happen. Similarly, I can only eat so much corn, and therefore I benefit from bartering away the extra amount. My best interest lies in others producing and prospering, as long as we communicate and barter together.

Allowing the opposite condition, a degenerating society, puts the survival of the individual at risk, and thus forcing him to act in society's interest. In other words, an individual and his relatives have a better overall chance at wealth in a wealthy society over a poor one, and also suffer a lesser risk of violence in a wealthy society. In general (but with dramatic exceptions), the poorer the society, the higher the state of political instability and personal insecurity. Therefore, being dependent upon society for survival (for food, security, shelter, information, etc.) and for happiness, the individual will largely act in generating overall societal wealth.

Although it is true that man prospers through a structured society, it is not necessary that he give up his freedoms as an individual to see society flourish. Exactly through greater personal freedoms will man be able to act in society's best interest, given the strong interdependence. Men do not die in patriotic fervor because they feel they are insignificant vis-à-vis their society and must, like an insect ,dedicate their lives to it. Instead they die because they feel they are only authenticated through freedom, a freedom attained through their structured society.

Free to Flow

To paraphrase Sartre, it is because of freedom and choice that we give meaning to our lives, and our world, through our actions. We are constantly redefining ourselves through the decisions we make and the paths we take, and it is only through the greatest freedoms that we can come closest to becoming whom we want and of whom we dream. Our history is a part of whom we are, largely because of the experiences that make it up, and the ensuing domino chains, relationships, and opportunities that accompany those experiences. Our choices are a critical component in the creation of those histories, and thus a critical component of the manufacturing of the self. And as we have discussed, it is through this creation or manufacturing of the self that meaning is derived as we fulfill our potentials to create value—value that is intrinsically derived but externally validated. Freedom thus plays an integral part in man's search for value and meaning as he walks the roads of life, and as he chooses among the forks on those roads. But just as freedom is essential to the creation of meaning, so is how we define freedom.

Traditionally, freedom meant the absence of obstacles, but here we have taken the existentialist point of view that freedom is the ability to overcome existing obstacles. The more obstacles there are, the more we know about those obstacles, and the greater our abilities to overcome them, the more freedom we have and the more material we have with which to define ourselves. In this book we went through a short, but significant list of obstacles. We started with internal obstacles, such as our instincts, emotions, and composite minds, and ended with external obstacles, such as death, subjective philosophical paradigms, and society. However, in general, the knowledge we possess is not what is important, since our store of knowledge will forever be tightly limited, but the idea that everything can and should be questioned. Only when we question do we reveal obstacles and allow ourselves to overcome them. Although we discussed the foundation upon which the majority of life's obstacles are built, more important to that was the goal of passing on the Socratic ideal of questioning everything thoroughly, to then learning from our questions and adapting our behaviors. Those foundational obstacles were revealed both as important insights into freedom and as examples of how to question life's experiences and our own understanding of those experiences.

We saw that some freedoms were more important than others depending on the individual and his value frameworks. In this sense limiting some freedoms and building some walls in order to concentrate essential time and energy on those things that are most important is rational. Some obstacles can and should be bigger than our abilities to overcome them, and should thus be bounded from our portfolio of choices. Not everyone can be an NBA player or Nobel prize winner, and not everyone should try. Internally, the mind tends toward chaotic thoughts and random patterns, necessitating a structure and a focus from which thoughts can flow. These structures are, of course, limitations to free thought, but they are also essential because of it.

The key, however, is to have the wisdom to know what is most important and what is not, so that the right structures can be chosen, and the right obstacles overcome. Man must begin with an open and free mind in order to fully create the image of his own identity, in spite of and in light of social biases, inherited prejudices, cultural tendencies, and habits in general. An open mind translates to the fully borne knowledge of the obstacles in life, their relative significance to the individual, and a responsible accounting of the repercussions and consequences of fighting and working to overcome them. It boils down to choosing the fights worth fighting, and picking the work worth enduring.

When we choose the most brutal fights and the most difficult work and apply our finest skills and talents to overcome them, we feel the most transcended. According to Csikszentmihalyi, we experience a sensation that he has dubbed "flow" when we engage in an activity that matches the level of difficulty of the activity to our inherent level of skill. It is during those moments that we feels things are clearest and the mind most uncluttered, when all actions are decisive, when awareness is heightened, when our concentration is only on the moment, and when we experience loss of self-consciousness and an altered sense of time. The experience takes on an artistic quality, where action is natural and beautiful. Flow is what the painter feels when creating a masterpiece, what the kids on the playground feel when playing basketball, what the banker feels when he makes money, what everyone feels when making love. It is being in the moment, feeling passion and intensity, letting go of all the anguishes of life, transcending all the absurdities of existence.

But not all flow experiences are the same. Csikszentmihalyi

describes flow at its most intense during those moments when challenges are highest and skills are at their utmost. Although level of difficulty in relation to skill level is a determinant of flow, so is absolute difficulty. The better and better someone can become at something, the more flow he experiences while taking on bigger and bigger challenges. The higher the skill level, the more intricate and complex the challenges, and the more beauty found in action. To go back to the example of the billiards player from Chapter Two, the player is probably going to feel more flow from playing the game than a beginner, taking on more difficult shots and becoming more focused on the moment. However, I say probably because determining flow involves a third factor—derived value. Someone might have a natural ability to play billiards and be very talented, but if he sees the game as pointless or as a waste of time, then he probably won't get much out of playing it.

In order to feel the most flow, we need to know ourselves well. We need to know what we do well and what we value in order to choose our activities and paths in life well. The better we know ourselves, the easier to choose things from which we derive the most fulfillment and flow. To not know ourselves well is to choose things that are too easy and boring for us, that do not add value to our lives, or that are insurmountable and frustrating. As Csikszentmihalyi says, the more an activity's difficulty supercedes our skills, the more stress and frustration we feel. If we cannot attain a goal that we have set for ourselves then we will never feel the satisfaction and sense of value from reaching it. Similarly, the more our skills supercede the challenge, the more boredom we feel. To do things that come easy is to not fulfill our potential. The trick is to choose goals that are slightly beyond our skills to ensure satisfaction and growth, but not too far beyond our skills where we feel stress and frustration.

Looking forward

As we discussed in the first two chapters, everyone has different valuation frameworks, and within those frameworks value is derived from breadth and depth of knowledge and experience. The more breadth and depth of experiences the more freedom is derived from greater choice and knowledge. In Chapter Seven we interpreted the value of this as translating into more domino chains with greater number of branches splitting off. Here, the tie to flow comes from the breadth and depth of skills that are derived. Skills are honed through depth, and thus the more experience in one area the greater the skills. Similarly, the broader the range, the greater the set of skills from which to choose. Thus with depth of skills we feel greater flow as we are able to meet challenges that are more difficult, while with breadth we have more opportunities to experience flow in our lives.

Life is full of obstacles to be overcome, and challenges to be met. As long as we allow ourselves the freedom, it is important that we choose those challenges that are most valuable to us and present us with the best opportunities to use our natural abilities and greatest skills. Not only will we feel the most fulfillment through the transcendental flow that is derived, but we and society at large will also gain the most value. Society gains the most when its members dedicate themselves to the activities at which they are most talented, given the economic theory of Comparative Advantages[55]. Man's sense of flow not only benefits him directly as he feels value from his contributions to society, but also indirectly through its derived benefit to society.

Now that we have given ourselves the freedom to create our own identities and go after the most meaningful obstacles, goals, and challenges, we need to give ourselves the freedom to overcome them. We will then feel fulfillment through this overcoming of goals. Facing the challenges we have set for ourselves can

---

[55] The theory of Comparative Advantages states that a group of individuals or nations are best off when they each dedicate their resources to producing those goods at which they are the most cost-efficient in producing relative to all other members, assuming free trade

be frightening because of the possibility of failure on the one hand, and success on the other, both of which will force us to evaluate the challenges we have chosen. The fear of meeting a challenge reverts back to the existentialist anguishes associated with freedom. If we fail, we have to entertain the possibility of having to choose again because of having chosen in error, not to mention all the angst that comes with failure. Similarly if we succeed, we have to choose again in order not to languish. Being is having to constantly redefine ourselves and thus having to continuously choose new goals and challenges. Having overcome those anguishes first in allowing ourselves the freedom to choose, we need to overcome them a second time in following through with our decisions.

But in overcoming these anguishes and choosing in full cognizance that the stories of our lives are written by us, and not despite us. Although the writing is irreversible and inexorable, we have seen that we posses full creative freedom over it; and as we embrace this freedom, we displace ignorance, its resulting regret, and its resulting misery.

We discussed and evinced the many influences that genetics and environment have over us, giving us the ability to map the paths that those influences take as they become our biases, prejudices, and mindsets. With a map in hand now, we can chart our own course towards principles as paradigms, rather than biases. Unremittingly, we must take on mental structures to navigate through our perceptual worlds to make decisions and act, but what is not a given is what paradigms are used. Principles are chosen and exist to guide us, where as biases are inculcated and they exist to push us. It is easy to see how we can come to regret that we allowed ourselves to be pushed, rather than having chosen to be guided, even if we come to the same decisions.

We embarked at the beginning of this book to reclaim our moral and existential freedoms by rooting out our old mental structures to create new ones. The knowledge we gained was important, but more important were the Socratic ideals of ques-

tioning motives and influences and the existential ideals of continuous regeneration of the self. I will let the reader be the judge
as to what was reclaimed. But the next time you come upon a
crucial decision remember to ask, "Am I leaning towards a decision, and why?" and, "Am I starting out with any assumptions
that may make me regret a decision, looking back five years from
now?"—in other words, "Why Freedom?"

References

Aronson, Elliot 1995. *The Social Animal, Seventh Edition*. New York, NY: W. H. Freeman and Company

Baynes, Kenneth; Bohman James; and McCarthy, Thomas 1991. *After Philosophy: End or Transformation?* Cambridge, MA: The MIT Press

Birney, Robert and Teevan, Richard C. 1961. *Instinct*. Princeton, NJ: D. Van Nostrand Company

Churchland, Patricia S. 1998, *Neurophilosophy: Toward a Unified Science of the Mind/ Brain*. Cambridge, MA: The MIT Press

Churchland, Paul M. 1999. *The Engine of Reason, the Seat of the Soul: A Philosophical Journey into the Brain*. Cambridge, MA: The MIT Press

Csikszentmihalyi, Mihaly 1993. *The Evolving Self: A Psychology for the Third Millenium*. New York, NY: HarperCollins

Damasio, Antonio R. 1994. *Descartes' Error: Emotion, Reason, and the Human Brain*. New York, NY: Avon Books

Dawkins, Richard 1989. *The Selfish Gene.* Oxford, England: Oxford University Press

Economist, Millennium Special Edition, December 31, 1999. "The end of urban man? Care to bet?", pgs. 25-26

Fletcher, Ronald 1966. *Instinct in Man: In the light of recent work in comparative psychology.* New York, NY: Schocken Books

Friedman, Milton & Rose 1980. *Free to Choose: A Personal Statement.* Orlando, FL: Harcourt Brace & Company

Goleman, Daniel 1997. *Emotional Intelligence: Why it can matter more than IQ.* New York, NY: Bantam Books

Gregory, Richard L., editor 1998, *The Oxford Companion to the Mind.* Oxford University Press

Gribbin, John 1984. *In Search of Schroedinger's Cat: Quantum Physics and Reality.* New York, NY: Bantam Books

Gribbin, John 1995. *Schroedinger's Kittens and the Search for Reality: Solving the Quantum Mysteries.* Toronto, Canada: Little, Brown, and Company

Griffin, Susan 1995. *The Eros of Everyday Life.* Doubleday books

Hayakawa, S.I. and Hayakawa, Alan R. 1992. *Language in Thought and Action.* Orlando, FL: Harcourt Brace & Company

Michalko, Michael 1998. *Cracking Creativity: The Secrets of Creative Geniuses.* New York, NY: Ten Speed Press

Nancy, Jean-Luc 1993. *The Experience of Freedom*. Stanford, CA: Stanford University Press

Olson, Robert G. 1962. *An Introduction to Existentialism*. New York, NY: Dover Publications

Searle, John R. 1998. *The Rediscovery of the Mind*. Cambridge, MA: The MIT Press

Wright, Robert 1994. *The Moral Animal: Why we are the way we are; The New Science of Evolutionary Psychology*. New York, NY: Vintage Books

Index

A

Abstraction. *See* See Emotions, Language
Aronson, Elliott 131
Artificial Intelligence 123, 141

B

Behaviorism 52, 130, 133
Biases and Prejudice 10, 31, 82, 235
    Bias 88

C

Camus, Albert 195, 206, 209
Chaos Theory 64
Churchland, Patricia 138
Churchland, Paul M. 136
Commissurotomy 138, 191
Comte, Auguste 175
Consciousness
    Cartesian Theater Theory of 134
    Domino Theory of 144
    Existentialism and 156, 188
    Frequency of 136
    Homunculus Theory of 134
    Levels of 137
    Neural Models of 140
    Schopenhauer and 153
    Synchronicity Theory of 135

F

Fairness, Concept of 33
Fletcher, Ronald 49, 53, 71, 150
Flow 235
Free will. *See* See Determinism
Freedom
  Existentialism and. *See* See Existentialism
  Knowledge and 119
  Liberty vs. 212
  Meaning and 118
  Meaning of 19, 20
  Moral 211
  Religion and 212, 218
  Responsibility and. *See* See
  Social importance of 37
  The Self and. *See* See Self, the
Freud, Sigmund 48, 53, 133

G

Goleman, Daniel 159
Goleman, Dr. Daniel 65, 67

H

Happiness 37, 41, 79, 80, 185
Heidegger, Martin 126
Heisenberg, Werner 177
Hobbes, Thomas 226
Hume, David 34, 78
Husserl, Edmund 155

I

Illusions, Visual 101
Instincts
  Behavior and 84, 145
  Definition of 49
  Evolution of 55
  Experience and 72, 149
  Fallibility of 75

N

Neural Hijacking 159
Newton, Isaac 21
Nietzsche, Friedrich 48, 117
Nothingness 42, 192, 193, 196
   Abstraction and 126, 127
   Anguish of Being and 108
   Consciousness and 154, 188

P

Parallel Distributed Processing 141, 143
Pascal, Blaise 209, 217
Pascal's Wager
   wager 209
Pavlovian Association 87
Philosophy
   Choice and 219
   Purpose of 111
   Science and 47, 180
Physics 176
   Newtonian 21
   Quantum 155, 177
Physiology. See See Instincts, Emotions
Plato 175
Pragmatism 34, 185
   Pragmatism 200
Probability Theory 182

R

Regret 12, 14, 194, 212
Religion
   Authority and 29
   Choice and
     religion 204
   History and 202
   Organization of 211, 222
Rousseau, Jean-Jacques 29, 58, 228, 231

S

T

U

V

Social 74
Time's inherent 36, 37, 207
Transcendental 113
Value System 237
Instinctual 64
Voltaire [Francois Marie Arouet] 34

W

Watson, John B.. *See* See Behaviorism
Wright, Robert 50, 52, 56

Printed in the United States
4491